Communication & Relationship

Match-made in Heaven

Awang Rozaimie

PARTRIDGE
A Penguin Random House Company

To order additional copies of this book, contact
Toll Free 800 101 2657 (Singapore)
Toll Free 1 800 81 7340 (Malaysia)
orders.singapore@partridgepublishing.com

www.partridgepublishing.com/singapore

Contents

Preface

Personal *cognitive* knowledge and *affective* interpersonal understanding are vital to sustain mutual and harmonic relationships, especially within a multiethnic society. As Malaysia has a diverse racial and ethnic composition, mutual intercultural understanding is crucial to avoid any potential intercultural conflict. The intention of this book is to describe basic knowledge of interpersonal communication so as to establish understanding and effective relations. The idea behind the book is to provide effective interpersonal communication strategies to institute beneficial interpersonal relations and communication. Specifically, the cognitive ideas, system and process in managing effective interpersonal relations and communication will be discussed in this book. Additionally, cross-cultural, intercultural and interethnic relations and interaction are sensitive and debatable issues in interpersonal communication. Thus, intercultural communication and understanding is emphasized in this book. We have kept the entire book straightforward and easy to read for any reader of various backgrounds. We hope you will enjoy reading it.

Acknowledgement

For completion of this book, heartiest dedication is directed to the Universiti Teknologi MARA, the organizations that the author represent, which provided venues and facilities to generate the idea of the book, as well as academic references. Great recognition is given to my family members, who were most passion and gave precious encouragement in the writing of this book. Respect to colleagues and friends, who contributed valuable sources, references and advice to polishing the contents of this book. Not forgotten are the others who directly or indirectly contributed ideas, comments and support to the accomplishment of this book

1 Introduction

"As to methods there may be a million and then some, but principles are few. The man who grasps principles can successfully select his own methods. The man who tries methods, ignoring principles, is sure to have trouble."—Ralph Waldo Emerson

Today, we live in a world of diversity and mobility of resources both daily and over an extended time continuum. Factors such as population, economic volatility, political stability, socio-cultural diversification, increase complexity of international relations. A recent report by the U.S. Census Bureau shows a 100% increase in the world's population, from three billion people in 1960 to six billion in 1999. Over the next 45 years, population is predicted to increase by another 100% from the current standing. The earth has 196.9 million sq miles surface area and approximately 70% of it is covered with oceans. This scenarios indicating that there is a limited inland space for someone to escape from interacting, communicating and creating relationships with other people.

We have to live and deal with people every days and nights. Each individual has different characters, emotions, intentions and perceptions that make interpersonal communication and relationship multifarious.

Thus, other important reasons for a person's are becoming involved in interpersonal communication and relationship are as follows:

1. ***Sophisticated communication.*** The speed and advancement of communications require people to interact and adapt to technological developments such as the usage of the Internet and fibre optics in sharing and transferring information. Other than advancement in communication gadgets, different human factors such as medical status, biological features and morale have turned interpersonal communication and relationshipinto a more complicated task. Each person conveys messages in different forms which are influenced by individual characteristics, features and backgrounds. Receiving, interpreting, retaining and responding to the transferring messages is a challenging task, especially without proper knowledge of the basic rules of interpersonal communication and relationshipsuch as: reading, writing, speaking and listening.

2. ***Sophisticated public.*** People are becoming more sensitive and aware of human issues and their implications on future life. Some examples include: global warming, green marketing and insider trading. In addition, a divergence in social relations such as a social stratification, status classes, hierarchy and ranking, may cause communal difficulties such as ethnocentrism, social bias, separation, discrimination and avoidance. A preventive solution to neutralize such social phenomena must be initiated promptly with mutually acceptable and harmonious mechanisms in order to avoid a future socially destructive generation. Additionally, a social convergence such as mixed-married and other interracial relationships indicates socio-cultural openness to establish a harmonious living.

3. ***Sophisticated information.*** *The Da Vinci Code (2006); The Code (2009);* and many other thriller movies are an entertaining way to show that the characteristics of information and messages can appear in many forms and channels for people to be involved in the encoding and decoding process. As people come with different perceptions, cultural backgrounds and education levels,

sufficient interpersonal skills and knowledge is highly required especially when conveying or demonstrating a technical message to these different people. For example, when a genealogical surgeon tries to explain the treatment of fertility to a chemical engineer; a mechanical engineer tries to demonstrate a proper use of fabrication machines to general workers and so forth.

4. ***Sophisticated creation and innovation.*** As many people become more educated, they challenge themselves to the maximum in order to fulfil their self-actualization needs. A saying: from the lowest point of the Dead Sea to the seven layers of the sky, there are mysteries and phenomena that call for explanation, need to be explored and measured, and have new research findings publicized and documented. Innovation is essential to improve future life and to test the limit of human potential. For example, the development of aerospace projects such as the Global Positioning System (GPS) satellites has been improved the speed and effectiveness of real-time broadcasting of information and communication around the globe. Technological advancement in communication is continuously moving towards a wireless and borderless world of communication and outer-space exploration.

Interpersonal communication and relationship are two broad and distinct, yet interrelated issues to discuss. Both interpersonal communication and relationship discuss similar but different systems and processes of connectedness. Examples connectivity systems and processes are self-concept and disclosure, perception, emotions, gender, listening, intimacy, symbols and representativeness, mode of communication, intercultural communication and conflict management. In addition, interpersonal relationship covers various systems of interaction that connect people, as well as organizations and businesses, which involve psychological, sociological, anthropological and spiritual understanding. Thus, the aim of this book is to convey general *rules of thumb* in effective interpersonal communication and relationship establishment.

2 Underlying Theories in Communication and Relationship

A theory is a set of concepts or ideas with explanations, assumptions, models, frameworks, axioms, propositions or hypotheses to describe the explicit (being influenced) and implicit (influencing other) phenomenon, behaviours, thoughts, emotions or perceived reality. A theory answers or explains what and how we know the thing has happened. In addition, a theory is posited or used based on accepted rational justifications, facts or evidence. Theory attempts to provide a plausible, rational and systematic explanation of the determinants, antecedents, factors, predictors or causal (cause-and-effect) relationships among observed samples (participants, representative or a portion of the observed population or subjects). A theory is explained or proposed by a thinker, researcher, philosopher or scholar (individual or group of people) who are experts in that particular area of psychology and human behaviour, and other scientific domains. Normally, sociological theories describe psychological behaviour and researchers will make appropriate interpretations, judgements and predictions about consequences, effects or future actions, responses and manners. We firmly believe that to communicate (to share, announce, inform or exchange) the meaning (ideas, perceptions and feeling) is the basis of relationship building. The effectiveness of message transmission is vital in interpersonal communication and relationship building. Thus, several prominent theories that explain the creations of interpersonal communication and relationship are shown in Table 2.1.

Table 2.1: Theories of Communication and Relationship

- Altman & Taylor's Social Penetration
- Argumentation Theory
- Attachment Theory
- Attribution Theory
- Berger & Calabrese's Uncertainty Reduction Theory
- Contagion Theories
- Classical Rhetoric
- Cognitive Dissonance Theory
- Dialectical Theory
- Elaboration Likelihood Model
- Equity Theory
- Expectancy Value Model
- Gibb's Supportive & Defensive Climates
- Goffman's Attenuation, Face Work, Impression Management
- Hall Dimensions of Culture
- Hart's Rhetorical Sensitivity
- Infante's Verbal Aggression
- Interpretative and Interaction Theories
- Knapp's Relational Stages
- Laing's Confirming and Disconfirming
- Laing's Spirals of Communication
- Language Expectancy Theory
- Lee's Love Types
- Maslow's Hierarchy of Needs
- Metacommunication
- Network Theory and Analysis
- Relational Dialectics
- Rule Theory
- Sapir & Whorf Linguistic Determination
- Self-Concept
- Self-Disclosure
- Self-Fulfilling Prophecy
- Self-Monitoring
- Self-Serving Bias
- Sensemaking
- Shutz's Interpersonal Needs Inclusion, Control, & Affection
- Social Cognition
- Social Cognitive Theory
- Social Comparison
- Social Exchange Theory
- Social Identity Theory
- Speech Act
- Spitzberg's Communication Competence
- Standpoint Theory
- Symbolic Interactionism
- System Theory
- Transactional Communication
- The Johari Window
- Theory of Planned Behaviour/ Reasoned Action
- Turning Points Theory
- Uncertainty Reduction Theory
- Vocate's Self-Talk
- Watzlawick, Beavin, & Jackson's Axioms of Communication
- Wilmot's Dyadic Communication

Source: Baxter & Braithwaite (2008)

However, the focus of this book only deals with the Theory of Interpersonal Needs and theories of relationships that will be discussed in the following sections.

THEORY OF INTERPERSONAL NEEDS

Basically, 'need' is a fundamental psychological, physiological and physical requirement of a human being, for living, satisfaction and life necessities. Abraham Maslow is a psychologist who first introduced a concept of human needs in his 1943 working paper entitled "A Theory of Human Motivation" and a book entitled "Motivation and Personality. Maslow (1943) suggests people are motivated to fulfil basic needs (lowest level) before moving on to the next level of need, sequentially, eventually achieving a more complex need at the top of the pyramid or hierarchy of need (as shown in the Figure 2.1). There are five levels of need: starting with physiological needs (basic), followed by safety (security), love/belongings (feeling, emotion), esteem (inner-self) and self-actualization (potential) as the highest need that humans are struggling to achieve.

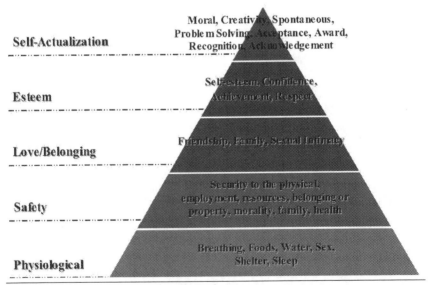

Figure 2.1: Maslow's Hierarchy of Needs

Moving on, according to Schutz (1991, 2005) in his Theory of Interpersonal Needs, there are three necessitates (needs) to fulfil for the creation of interpersonal relationships. The interpersonal needs include an inclusion, control and/or affection to which connectedness is created through expressing and/or wanting process.

1. ***Inclusion*** is a process during which we include ourselves with the others to be part or member of their group, association, club, community or society. The inclusion process can include forming new relations; reuniting with long lost friends; creating feelings of belonging; participating in an event; being noticed or being visible before others. Some people express an inclusion by approaching or reaching out to the others in welcome; walking up to a group of people; writing memos; or calling or texting a message by cellular phone. On the other hand, some people look for inclusion by hoping, wondering or waiting for somebody to approach them by calling, texting, greeting or inviting someone to start the conversation or join the group.

2. ***Control*** is a process in which we have power over someone's actions or manipulate them to guide us about some job or actions. People express a control by initiating some movement by praising, suggesting, influencing, leading, rebelling, commanding, confronting, excelling or being seen as competent. On the other hand, some people initiate control by applying, requesting or asking for help, opinion, advice, or by empowering the other to make a decision.

3. ***Affection*** is a process in which we express a feeling or emotion (sign, notice, love, pity, like, admire, fondness, warmth, friendliness, care) or desire such responses from them. Affection is created by initiating or developing authentic relationships and responses that are close, open and warm. Some people express affection by complimenting, praising, touching, winking, whistling, prolonged eye contact, smiling, laughing or crying. On the other hand, some people encourage affection by giving a clue on his/her desire to have something, hinting at a gift, prolonged eye contact, desiring, praying for or nurturing others.

THEORIES OF RELATIONSHIPS

A relationship is a human connectedness, chemistry or networking created with reason or by coincidence. Hence, a beneficial relationship is established with mutual acceptance and understanding between parties who are involved in the process. There are five groups of relationships including society, social communities, individual and relationship processes; that will be discussed in the following sections.

Societal Relationship

Society is a human association or group of people who communicate, commute, live and/or work in a place, village, residential or industrial area (urban, suburb or rural), settlement, park, town, city, state, country or region. People in a society may share a traditional or corporate culture (belief, norms, values and attitudes), political structure, socio-economic and other socio-cultural aspects (such as religion, material possession, custom, language, dialect, routine, and behaviour). A theory of *Symbolic Interaction* posited by George Herbet Mead (Mead, 1934 in Blumer, 1966) in his book "Mind, Self and Society" has explained that relationship between people in the society is established through a representation of the messages in the interaction processes.

Symbolic interaction is an ability of the people to interact using particular words, signs, movements and gestures that represent meanings (ideas, feelings, and perceptions) to convey the messages. Sets of vocabulary, clauses, phrases and sentences will create a language that represents the identity or culture of the particular society. Dialect, accent and slang are phonetic effects that may also differentiate the identity of different societies. For example, by listening to the accent we could probably differentiate between a Bristol, American, Aussie and Kiwi. The ability to rearrange symbols into words is based on the mental frame of references projected in our minds. The frame of references is created through self observation, past experiences, being taught by other people or self judgments. Thus, the three elements that connect or label people and their behaviours or actions are meaning (intention), language and thought (Mead, 1934) through their social interaction.

Social Communities

Community is a fraction of the society. Community is formed based on peoples' interest, hobbies, activities, expertise, housing area, products or services consumption and so forth. The particular community is established for non-profit purposes or striving for certain aims such as human rights, green environment and peace. Two theories explain formations of social communities: Standpoint Theory and Attachment Theory.

1. ***Standpoint Theory*** posited by Georg William Fredrick Hegel (Hegel, 1971) in his "The Cider House Rules" which stressed that human relationship are established due to the creation of culture, heritage, families, experiences and expectations. As in the "security need" in Maslow's Hierarchy of needs, a person may feel insecure, hopeless or lonely by standing alone or without others in support. To fulfil the need for security, people search for others to provide support, advice, guidance or protection. Thus, a community is established among people (whom they like, trust, are similar, connected to or have chemistry with) for particular purposes, reasons or gifted. However, to accommodate these needs, relationships among colleagues, teams, groups or societies are sometimes established due to the differences in power, opportunities, and perspectives. Different groups will shape particular members' experiences, knowledge, skills, understanding, and ways of interacting, communicating or relating.

2. The magnitudes of relatedness, connectivity, integration, relationship or association between peoples are explained by the ***Attachment Theory.*** The Attachment Theory was posited by John Bowlby and Mary Ainsworth (Bowlby, 1998; Bowlby & Ainsworth, 1991) in which the relationship is created according to the inception level between the Model of Self and Model of Other. The theory is explained through the Attachment Model as shown in the Figure 2.2.

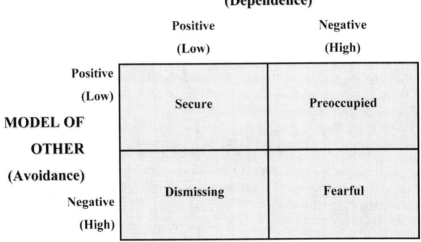

Figure 2.2: Attachment Model

Relationship creation is depending on the magnitude of closeness, relatedness, trust, belief, norms and distance of the attachment between people, groups or society. In the Model of Self, people think and worry about themselves. In addition, people think and worry about their relationships pictured in the Model of Other.

The Model of Self indicates the magnitude of a person being dependent. Knowledge and skills, maturity, personality and appropriate frame of references help an individual to make wise and precise decisions, and behave appropriately. However, to grow and achieve higher levels of needs as a human being, a person is dependent on many other factors, such as: availability of resources, social support and a conducive physical surrounding. People will act positively if their level of dependence is low and in contrast, a higher level of dependence shows negative relationships between people. Thus, an individual's positive or negative behaviour is also determined by the Model of Other.

The Model of Other indicates the level of avoidance towards a person: whether to accept, reject, keep or maintain the relationship. The lower level of the other's avoidance, the more positives the relationship is. Similarly, the higher level of the other's avoidance, the more negatives the magnitude of relationship between people.

In addition, there are four types of relationships: secure, preoccupied, dismissive and fearful.

a. The relationship is *secure* with both positive Model of Self and Model of the Other. A mutual relationship is created when a person has a lower level of dependency and a lower level of avoidance by the others. A secure relationship is the most favourable, mutual and beneficial relationship as both parties (a person and the other) are showing all positive personality traits such as openness, empathy, flexibility and so forth.

b. *A Preoccupied* relationship is created when an individual has a negative model of self but a positive model of the other. A person may grow only with support by the other (higher level of dependence) and at the same time people may need, respect or accept a person (lower level of avoidance) due to certain reasons such as kinship, socio-political or economic benefits or religion. For example, autism, downs-syndrome or paralyzed children; group leaders, priests or imams.

c. A positive Model of Self, but negative Model of Other will create a *dismissing* relationship. Dismissing relationships occur when a person with a lower level of dependency would like to establish a relationship, but the other might resist or reject the proposal as they have a higher level of avoidance. This scenario happens probably when a person has a previous negative record of betraying friendship, is a dictatorial type of person, or has other hygienic or psychological problems.

d. A loneliness or *fearful* relationship happens when there is both negativity in the Model of Self and Model of Other. Fearful relationships occur when a person has a high level of dependency, and the other has a high level of avoidance. A fearful feeling or relationship happened as both sides (individual and the other) are afraid to establish a relationship, probably because of security or health reasons. For example, a person probably involved in crime, having mental problems or having acute and infectious diseases.

As a result, isolation and annoyance behaviour are portrayed either by one or both people.

Additional to the Attachment Model as shown in the Figure 2.2, the relationship between a person and the other could also be explained using the radar as in Figure 2.3. There are two fundamental methods to explain people's differences, according to the way they might think about relationships. The magnitude of attachment or relationship building is dependent on the level of avoidance (Y-axis) and anxiety level (X-axis). Anxiety is a psychological effect in which people feel afraid, unsure or take extra precautions before doing something or making a decision. In the Attachment Model, low levels of avoidance and anxiety will establish a *secure* relationship. The relationship is *preoccupied* with low avoidance but high anxiety. *Dismissing-Avoidant* relationship is created by a low level of anxiety but high level of avoidance. Lastly, *Fearful-Avoidant* relationship is produced by a high level of anxiety and avoidance.

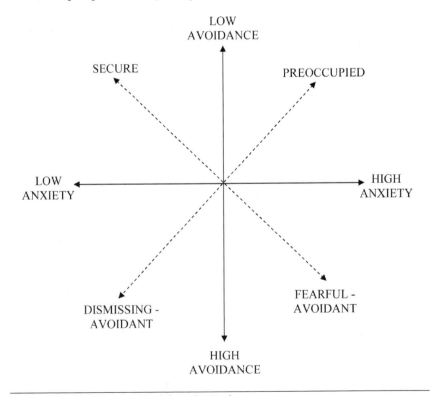

Figure 2.3: Attachment Model in the Radar

Notably, some people are more anxious than others, and some are more avoidant than others. Anxiousness or avoidance behaviour is depending on people's intention or goals in the relationship creation. Those who score higher in attachment-related anxiety are concerned about others. They tend to worry about the worth of the relationship and be fearful of rejection. On the other hand, those who score higher in attachment-related avoidance are concerned about their self comfort zone and personal space. Openness to others depends on the other's personality, need for attachments or relationships, and other factors.

Individual

As an individual or a person, we are acting in a 'self' system determines satisfaction or fulfils expectations when dealing with relationship building or communication. In communication, the individual as a unit is responsible for message creation or interpreting the received message into an appropriate form. Elements of communication (intrapersonal, interpersonal, informational and decisional) will be discussed in a later chapter. Thus, sufficient and effective communication is vital in order to establish mutual and beneficial relationships. A **Social Cognition** or a **Personal Construct Theory** by George Kelly (Kelly, 1955) explained the fundamental ways a person as an individual unit establishes the relationship, accepting or rejecting the others, or behaves in a particular manner.

Psychological reactions or cognitive recognitions establish a "construct". As an individual, a construct is a mental audio-visual projection or messages (ideas, intentions and perceptions). Past experiences, frame of references, environment and health issues help to define a construct of social connectedness, networking or relationship. A construct may comprise several factors or interdependent elements. For example, when we meet a person (a construct) several issues may arise such as his/her name, age, religion, ethnicity, education level, job, origin, nationality and so forth. Particularly, certain magnitude of emotions, feelings, behaviours and other responses are dependent on the six construct developments as discussed in the following section.

1. *The direct definition.* People act or behave impromptu according to the need for reactions or behave at the time they need to give direct or indirect responses. In certain situations, such as in an

emergency, people will define the scenarios directly without any further analysis or requesting of additional information for decision making. For example, while driving when we see the traffic light change from yellow to red, we react promptly by stopping the car at the junction.

2. *Reflected appraisals.* While being asked, receiving or hearing any statement or phrases, we analyze the content of the message before taking required actions or giving particular responses. For example, when hear the order "close the door", we might think and appraise several actions to take: such as which, when, why and how to close the door. Impromptu actions take place for repetitive actions or when we have experience of doing or making similar decisions. Mental reflections such as: should or should not, just or unjust, appropriate or not, cost and benefit or other possible consequences; are influenced by many factors such as experience, knowledge and skill to react appropriately.

3. *Identity scripts.* In an occasion when we meet people, especially new or unfamiliar people, we might try to recall or analyze the character of a person before making necessary communication, conversation, connection or relationship. In such event, a mental register or frame of references is important to identify any possible clues to recognize a person. Some people believe their heart-feeling or sixth sense before making a move or action to greet, talk, converse or connect with others. Early assessment is crucial to avoid any possible danger, harassment, annoyance or other unfavourable behaviours.

4. *Prototypes.* Prototypes are the other elements incorporated before connecting or creating relationships with others. We are probably going to search for similarities or compare a new person we meet with somebody else (possibly correlated). For example, we try to connect a person that we meet for the first time with somebody else, such as his/her close friends, family members (parents, siblings, husband/wife, or children), neighbours or work colleagues that we are already familiar with. We then make an early judgement on the personality or character of that person

and his/her intention based on referent before making further connection, conversation or relationship.

5. *Personal constructs.* In an occasion when we have no clue about the others, or meet the strangers in a new environment without past experience or appropriate frame of reference, it is vital for us to take extra precautions to avoid any possible danger such as harassment, deception, rape or snatches. We will make a personal assessment or judgment about a person that we meet before making further connections, conversations or relationship. Thus, it is important for us to take necessary and appropriate ice-breaking actions by asking questions to assess the personality of a person, such as ascertaining their hobby, origin, and other academic and socio-cultural background information (such as race, ethnic background and religion). However, to create early rapport with strangers, self-awareness is important to avoid asking about sensitive issues, such as criminal history or experience, sexual or intimate relationships, and respecting the other's personal space and privacy.

6. *Stereotypes.* Some people make easy assessments or judgements by using stereotypes about others. Sometimes, a stereotype is able to assist creating beneficial relationships with others. For example, a man wearing smart attire, driving an expensive vehicle, escorted by a personal bodyguard and/or only appearing occasionally must be an important person (VIP) for his/her particular organization, society or nation. Thus, when communicating with VIP, we would make appropriate preparation in, for example, appearance, manners, etiquette and protocol. However, stereotypes could create danger that may cause interpersonal and intercultural conflict. For example, it is a racial danger by saying a general stereotype "Chinese are greedy (*Kiasu*), Indians are cheaters and Malays are lazy". Certainly, those stereotypes are faulty in today's competitive living. People of any socio-cultural and demographic background can achieve the highest level of success, depending on self willingness, effort and initiative to excel and obtain particular knowledge and skills.

To conclude, Kelly (1955) stressed that we, as a person or an individual, accept or entertain certain 'things' only when 'something' is perceived as meaningful and beneficial to us. People could deny, reject or annoy those things that are unfavourable, hurtful, and difficult to achieve or make a loss. Besides, people will act, react or make decisions effectively only when familiar with the environment, task, or job; or have a sufficient personal frame of reference and are positive in their mind-set. Additionally, mutual relationships are created and people can understand other people better when their mental or psychological systems have a chemistry or similarity.

Relationship Processes

There are systems or processes involved in creating mutual and beneficial relationships.

1. ***System Theory.*** System theory stresses the concepts of interdependence and wholeness or mutual influence in communication and relationships. As a system, there are several sequential activities starting from input, followed by processes and ending with the result or output as shown in Figure 2.4. An example of the system is the digestive system in a body. According to Whitchurch and Constantine (1993) there are four elements that establish an effective system, discussed as in the following:

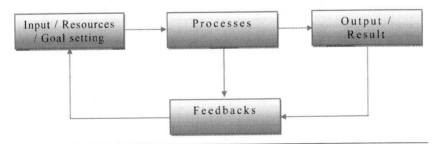

Figure 2.4: System Approach

    a. *Equifinality* is an ability, reliability and functionality of a system to achieve the planned goal, although using different methods or routes. For example, there are many ways to get more money, such as investment, savings, borrow from other or involve in business. Every method has different tenure, rules, procedures, and disciplines in order to achieve the similar goal: to get more money. Setting achievable goals is crucial to ensure the effectiveness of the system. The feedback loops along the process are important to ensure the operation of the systems is on the right track and improve the effectiveness of goal achievement.

b. There are *hierarchies* in a system, depending on the complexity of the process and goal settings. Layers, red tape or barriers, rules, procedures, protocols and levels in the systems increase complexity, tenure and goal attainment. For example, when organizing a musical concert, there are subsystems that support the big event (the musical concert as a whole is a system). Thus, in order to ensure the success of the musical concert, there are several subsystems that support the process, such as sound systems, stage management, floor systems (audience arrangement, security, ticketing) and so forth. In addition, larger and most complex systems are known as supra-systems. A nation involves many subsystems of economic, political, social and security systems. However, there are difficulties to determine appropriate sub-systems and their components to ensure the effectiveness of activities execution, assignments, and empowerments, and to avoid work or job overlapping and conflict of interest.

c. It is difficult for system establishment to identify appropriate *boundaries*. The boundaries comprise power, responsibility, authority and the jobs which will determine the membership of a system, chain of command or line of authority. The boundaries also determine a connection between subsystems or with other systems. However, the boundaries vary in complexity, control and flow of work, responsibility, authority and power within and between the systems and/or its subsystems. For example, a system of family in which the distance of kinship, status, health and wealth determines emotional and psychological connectedness between family members. In addition to the boundaries as above, there are open and/or closed forms of systems which determine the flexibility of the systems. *Open systems* permit the interferences and openness of the systems. Additional subsystems are allowed to exist alongside the execution process of the system. For example, a newly married family member adds the new subsystems to the existing system of family. In contrast, *closed systems* control or obstruct interference in the system. For example, court jurisdiction in Malaysia is an example of a closed system which does not allow media broadcasting or the public (without permission) to attend or follow the proceedings.

d. In order to assure the effectiveness of the systems, control and feedback are two important elements that permit correction, advancement, enhancement and improvement of the system. We need to control the systems to ensure that procedures and work executions are on track or as planned. Appropriate and sufficient feedback's control unwelcome interferences to jeopardise the goal. For example, in a marriage we should not allow third parties or unrelated individuals to decide what the husband and wife should do, except for giving advice or suggestions.

In addition, the feedback loop allows reassessment to improve the system effectiveness. A feedback loop is a path in a system that exists in the middle or at the end of the communication process. The feedback loop could get hold of the process if there are possible effects, malfunctions, problems or if the outputs are not as planned or expected. The appropriate suggestion for improvement, correction, advancement or replacement is obtained through the appropriate negotiations, discussion, and "muzakarah" or "usrah" session. The feedback is considered positive or negative according to the effect it has on the system. Moreover, the feedback (negative or positive) depends on the receiver's message interpretation, intentions, feelings and expectation. *Negative feedback* is used to maintain the status-quo or homeostasis which maintains the consistency of the system. Maintaining a homeostasis feedback has also been called constancy loops and deviation-attenuating loops. For example, peaceful discussion heart-to-heart is useful to solve any quarrel between husband and wife. Besides, there are negative loops known as morphostatic feedback which promote the maintenance of the existing structure of the systems. For example, candle-light dinner or gift giving is reasonable to solve any quarrel between husband and wife.

Positive feedback is used to promote change or permit replacement. Positive feedback has also been referred to as deviation-amplifying loops or variety loops. For example, taking a vow during a wedding anniversary or vacation is a choice to ensure that marriage relationships are continuous. The changes to the structure of the system are referred to as morphogenic feedback. For example, child adoption is a choice for the problem of a childless married couple.

In addition to the system theory as above, Watzlawick, Beavin and Jackson (1967) posited an ***interactional view*** of a communication process and relationships building. In an interactional view, there are several reasons to start the process of communication, interaction, conversation, networking or building relationships.

a. It is almost impossible for a person not to communicate, either to him/herself or with others. There are types, processes and methods of human communication which vary from whispering to verbal or nonverbal communication (this will be discussed in a later chapter).
b. Communication comprises content or messages (ideas, perceptions, intentions or feelings) and relationship. Messages are created, exchanged and shared with those who are connected, targeted or expected to receive them.
c. The relationship establishment, depth, magnitude and frequency depends on how, and the extent to which, both parties (sender and receiver, speaker and listener) interrupt,

punctuate, arrange or engage in the communication sequence.

d. Communication in a relationship is symmetrical, complementary or parallel. Firstly, symmetrical communication relationships are created when both parties have similar messages to exchange in two-way or face-to-face communication. Symmetrical communication requires honesty, respect and effort to achieve mutual understanding between two parties. Secondly, communication relationships are complementary when prompt feedback, responses or actions are not required, such as an advertisement, announcement or reading materials. Lastly, parallel communication occurs by stages, or single messages following one after another. Parallel communication allows complex messages to be effectively conveyed in steps or by particular procedures.

2. **Social Exchange Theory.** Thibaut and Kelly (1952, 1959) posited the Social Exchange Theory in which people are engaged in a relationship for exchange of returns, benefits or rewards, and costs. Worth or outcomes of the relationship created are obtained after extracting any possible costs or risks from rewards received. For example, marriage is arranged after taking into consideration barriers, risks or costs (such as time, effort, expenditure, objections, problems, separation) from possible rewards (such as happiness, companionship, social support, monetary sharing, and family expansion). Although worth of relationship is difficult to calculate mathematically, there are values and beliefs that could be taken into consideration in the establishment of a relationship. The goal in relationship creation is to maximize rewards and minimize costs towards the perceived possible outcomes of beneficial relationships. In particular, social behaviour is the result of an exchange process. When the outcome is perceived greater, people tend to disclose more information, share secrets, and develop closer or intimate relationships with trusted individuals or people. In contrast, when expected risks outweigh the rewards, people tend to terminate, abandon or ignore the relationship.

3. ***Dialectical Theory.*** The theory posited by Leslie Baxter and Barbara Montgomery (Baxter & Montgomery, 1996; Montgomery & Baxter, 1998) explained that relationship is created and established based on the contradictory elements of a system. Contradictory elements refer to the dynamic forces between unified opposites which are actively incompatible. Incompatible elements in a system somehow are interdependent with each other and create a relational system. There are three relational dialectic dimensions: integration/separation, stability/change and expression/privacy. In addition, the contradictory forces that occur in a relationship are based on either internal tensions or external tensions.

  a. *Internal tensions.* There are inner forces of a person that turn the needs for a relationship to a certain level or magnitude of attachment.

    i. Autonomy/Connection. Autonomy is the need to be independent or have a certain level of freedom, power or authority. In contrast, some people prefer closeness, networking or relatedness as a reason to establish the relationship. In certain circumstances, autonomy and connection go parallel to gain trust, respect and social support.

    ii. Predictability/Novelty. In certain conditions, establishment, effect or consequences of the relationship is predictable. For example, an intimate relation between a man and woman might end up with marriage or companionship. In contrast, some relationships are established naturally or by "force of nature" such as a kinship, day and night and so forth.

    iii. Openness/Closedness. A dynamic or open relationship is expandable when people are allowed to join, participate, withdraw, or terminate the membership based on preferences, understanding or interest. However, membership by selection, invitation, or special interest indicates closeness of the relationship to certain goals, intentions, preferences, values, norms or beliefs.

b. *External tensions.* There are outer forces of a person that turn the needs for a relationship to a certain level or magnitude of attachment.

   i. Inclusion/Exclusion. Similarities, interests, intentions and preferences force some people to be included in the membership of groups, teams or society. However, different knowledge, goals, status, ranking, hierarchy or other social-cultural background exclude some people from the group.
   ii. Conventionality/Uniqueness. Membership of the group, team or society is created based on the common interest, location, events or activities. On the other hand, exclusive relationships are established according to specific themes, expertise, interests, goals or kinship, such as a family that creates uniqueness of the identity of the particular group.
   iii. Revelation/Concealment. In certain circumstances, a relationship is established to reveal, inform, announce, expand or share an image, identity, interest, knowledge, skills, information, assets, property, belongings or possessions. On the other hand, a 'underground', secret or exclusive group, team or club is created to preserve or protect an image, identity, interest, knowledge, skills, information, assets, property, belongings or possessions.

4. ***Turning Points Theory.*** The theory posited by Laub, Nagen and Sampson (1998) discussed the feelings towards the events, system or processes that a person perceives as the new direction, order or plan. There are several influential events interrelated to the positive or negative changes happening in the relationship. The changes are important to ensure that improvement, advancement or correction is properly made towards the initial goal's

achievement. There are four events or dimensions which create changes in the relationship.

a. *Dyadic* influence shows the basic reasons for the interaction. For example, having a fight or quarrel, getting engaged, pregnancy and so forth.
b. *Individual* factors form the basis that creates personal belief systems. For example, insufficient savings, being too young to marry, too ambitious, lacking knowledge or skills, being the wrong shape to be a model.
c. *Network* indicates interference or connectedness with third parties that contribute to the interaction process. For example, parental or board of director approval, disapproval of his/her siblings and so forth.
d. *Circumstantial* effects happen due to unpredictable or out-of-control events. For example, a natural disaster, bankruptcy, relocation and so forth.

At the time when the relationship is not working, people need to realise the causes of uncertainty or difficulty. A moment to reassessing the relationship is known as the turning point. Acknowledge the mistake and conceive the solutions are the best solution to the interpersonal relationship and communication violence. It is important to a person not to repeat the same mistake in the future. Getting support from the third parties (such as spouse, friends and family) are able to help individual to sense any signals to the changes in the relationship.

3 Effective Communication and Relationship

Referring to the chicken and egg metaphor, which should come first? Is it a relationship? or communication? The answer should depend on the needs, demands and reasons for interaction. Basically, interpersonal communication is defined as the process of transmitting information from one person to another. Once communication is created, interpersonal relations will be established. This involves a human connection to fulfil the need or to accomplish a personal or non-personal motive. Some people connect with others for intimate, familial, friendship, support, avoiding loneliness and other personal motives. Some other people create relationships with the others known as customers, clients, patients and so forth, with non-personal motives or reasons, such as establishing a business network, gaining profits, and/or due to their job dealing with people. Thus, effective communication would establish chemistry (connectedness or relationships).

ELEMENTS OF COMMUNICATION

A beneficial relationship is established with mutual acceptance and understanding between parties who are involved in the process. Particularly, communication involves four elements consisting of: an intrapersonal, interpersonal, decisional and informational mode of interaction, as shown in Figure 3.1.

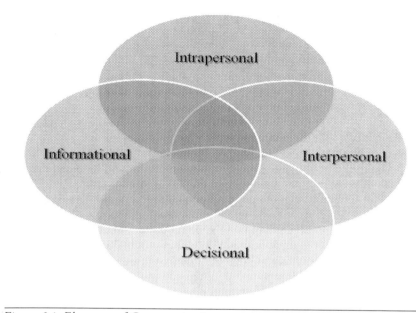

Figure 3.1: Elements of Communication
Source: Author

1. ***Intrapersonal communication*** is a process of self-realization, self-assessment and self-awareness within a person. In silence, people perform self analysis; or debate with themselves in their mind about some event, idea, and wish; or assess other people's behaviour, appearance or actions. Intrapersonal communication is also exist in a form of *monologue* (is a recitation in which a person talks to himself) which may direct or assist in decision making. Intrapersonal responses are a method of reflecting, judging and fulfilling self-need, want, desire, and expectation. Every person has an exclusive set of beliefs, norms, perceptions and other particular *frames of reference* before expressing an action, behaviour or opinion. For example, before attending an interview, we might consider what appropriate garments to wear (type, size, colour, and fashion); how long the interview will take; the nature of the interviewers (personality, background, job position); possible questions to be asked by the interviewer; and result of the interview.

2. ***Interpersonal communication*** involves an interaction with other people in order to fulfil pre-determined desires and needs. It is important for a person to realize a purpose, cause and implication of the communication that they have started. Therefore, it is necessary to acquire knowledge and skills about the art of communication such as: process, procedures, rules and regulations, methods, message transmission vehicles, medium or channels, taboos, and environmental screening, in order to establish mutually effective communication and its benefits.

3. ***Decisional communication*** is a process in which a person seeks information to use for decision making and to communicate the research findings. An efficient organizational decisional tree is a critical element in business communication because every decision is probably about money (cost and profit), effective leadership and business strategy. At an individual level, decision is about satisfaction, moral or social value and avoiding disappointment with the responses, outcomes and effects. For example, making a decision either to buy 2011 BMW 5 series or 2011 Audi A8. Thus, making appropriate and wise decisions is crucial to avoid regret or disappointment and business fraud, such as misuse of information, insider trading, confiscation or bankruptcy.

4. ***Informational communication*** is the process of acquiring and disseminating information for individual or general use. Informational communication is about evaluating the usage of data, and gathering or spreading information which has social, economic and cultural impact. Sufficiency, accuracy, coherence and usefulness of content of the information, all have an interaction and relations impact when the message is transmitted to other people. A prompt feedback is not expected in informational communication where the messages are transmitted through printed advertisement (such as brochure, flyers, pamphlet and billboard) or broadcasting Medias (such as television, radio and internet). Example communicating information includes: announcing the new opening of a store, launching a new product, changing business location, publishing

a new book, making an appointment, writing an obituary or condolences, advertising job vacancies and so forth.

A crucial aspect of human interaction is to gain the positive impact of an effective communication. Effective communication involves a process of sending or transmitting a message, in which the received message is decoded with the interpreted meaning being as the message intended. 'Meaning' is the ideas, intentions or reasons for a particular communication being received as the sender intended (Lewis, Goodman & Fandt, 2001). An effective communication process involves a complete cycle in which a person (source) sends a signal or transmits a message to another person (receiver) through appropriate channels, as shown in Figure 3.2.

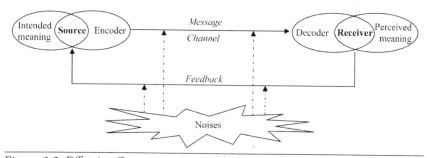

Figure 3.2: Effective Communication and Relationship Building
Source: Lewis, Goodman and Fandt (2001)

1. A **source** (speaker, writer, author) will encode the **intended meaning** (something to inform, teach, explain, acknowledge) to be communicated into a message form (verbal or non-verbal) that can be transmitted to the **receiver** (listener, audience, reader). The **messages** (ideas, intentions, perceptions, feelings and opinions) will be **encoded** into a signals, symbols or words which represent the meaning (connotation, sense) and should be transferable or interpretable by the receiver. The various forms of messages will be discussed further in the following chapter.

2. The **message** is transmitted through a **channel** or a vehicle to carry the message either in verbal, non-verbal or written form. An appropriate selection of media, medium, channel, vehicle or

method to transfer the message is a crucial aspect in order to establish a complete cycle of effective communication. According to Kagan (1972), using visible modes, such as videotape and other audio-visual devices with proper guidance, instruction or demonstration, are reliable and efficient methods of establishing effective communication. Communication aid especially the audio-visual devices (such as the Compact Disc (CD), an optical disc of Dissociated Vertical Deviation (DVD), the Moving Picture Experts Group (MPEG-1) or (MPEG-2) Audio Layer III or IV (known as MP3, MP4), Skype, Twitter, emails Messenger and so forth) is reliable when communicating a complex message and between people in separate locations.

3. Once the receiver has noted or received the communication signal, the receiver will **decode** the message into a **perceived meaning** (receiver's intentions that are interpreted in a way the receiver understands). With the same process used in sending the message, the receiver will decode the verbal or non-verbal signals, symbols or words that he/she has received which are intended to represent the meaning that the sender wished to convey. The message acceptance is dependent on the ability of the receiver to interpret the message into his/her understandable form. This process may be influenced by: the quality of the transmitted message; use of appropriate channels; and the receiver's biological or environmental factors. Effective communication is achieved when the messages received by the receiver are accurate, and when sender and receiver have similar ideas, perceptions, feelings, intentions and opinions.

4. A complete communication cycle requires **feedback** or a response by the receiver as a signal of acceptance. A feedback loop or response will probably appear in verbal or non-verbal forms, signals, symbols or words, in order to react, accept, reject, modify and/or expand the meaning of the transmitted message. Feedback or responses might exist *impromptu* or in time according to the needs, accessibility, necessities, message complexity, distance, relation and status between sender and receiver. In certain conditions, the sender will make an assumption about the success

of the message transmitted to the target or receiver due to lack of feedback or response (usually a sign of rejection or disagreement). For example, when carrying out a mail survey which has unreturned questionnaires, the researcher will assume that the respondent did not agree to participate in the survey, although there is the possibility that the questionnaire could be lost, due to default by the mail service provider. Besides, feedback is not expected or required *impromptu,* especially in an informational communication. For example, advertisements (such as sales promotions) and announcements, to which the results, reactions, feedback or replies are expected sometime in the future.

5. In addition, there will be **noises** or interference in the communication process. 'Noises' are interruptions that may hamper the communication process. Noises occur in the form of: physical distractions, semantic problems, status effects, demographic issues, religious influences, knowledge understanding, information overloads, incorrect channels, emotions, cultural influences and absence of feedback. Noises could modify, change, obliterate or detour the transmitted message or feedback.

TYPES OF INTERPERSONAL RELATIONSHIP

Consequently, a completed cycle or effective communication will lead to the effective establishment of relations. Effective relations are an art of creating beneficial relationship, intimacy, connectivity, trust, respect and other chemistry between two or more people. There are various forms, of interpersonal relations establishment, such as kinship, marriage, and formal and informal forms of humans association.

1. **Kinship** is a human relationship based on familial relatedness. Kinship or immediate families are connected by genetics. Every level of kinship association is determined by age and magnitude of respect given or received. Kinship members include grandfather and grandmother, father and mother, brother and sister, son and daughter, grandson and granddaughter, uncle and aunt, cousin, and nephew and niece.

2. **Marriage** refers to peoples' connectivity which is formed with permission from the particular legal authority. A man and woman who do not have a kinship relationship are allowed to build an intimate personal relationship as husband and wife, living permanently together through the legal arrangement of marriage. In addition, people known as in-laws are connected to the whole family members' of his/her partner by marriage (such as father-in-law, mother-in-law, brother-in-law, sister-in-law and so forth). From the religious point of view, Islam allows a man to legally marry four women (each of them without kinship relationship) if he can ensure he is able to treat all his wives without any discrimination of love physically, financially, psychologically and emotionally. Recently, current controversial laws in Western countries (such as in several states in the United States of America, Denmark, the United Kingdom of Great Britain, Canada, and Brazil) allow a couple of Lesbian, Gay, Bisexual and Transgender (LGBT) to be legally married, in civil unions or register partnerships. These laws challenge accepted conventional religious teachings.

3. In certain conditions, people connect to others based on their **formal** social relationship. A formal rapport is created at school (kindergarten, primary, secondary, high), college, university, club or society, workplace, meeting, seminar, conference, forum, summit, and so forth. Formal relationship exist with a *line of authority* or magnitude of decisional power, based on their designation as an executive, teacher, lecturer, officer, managing director, engineer, doctor, lawyer, clerk and so forth. Reasons for a formal relationship are: career advancement, job requirement, sustaining business or organizational networking, work enforcement and execution. In addition, formal relationships among people are also based on the social status, being **awarded** by a country's highest authority such as King, Queen, Governor or President. A recipient of royal recognition, orders of knighthood, medals of honour or honorary awards will brings titles such as: Knight (KG/KT), Lady (LG/LT), Knight/Dame Cross (GBE), Knight/Dame Commander (KBE/DBE), Commander (CBE), Officer (OBE), Member (MBE), Tun, Tan

Seri, Datuk Seri, Datuk, Dato; and have certain magnitude of pride, respect, power, social status and hierarchy within a society.

4. A close relationship can also be established through an **informal** social relationship or connectivity. Informal rapport is created when people are dating or meeting in situations such as: social parties, clubs, neighbours, social websites (such as Facebook, Twittter and blog), restaurants, coffee shops, shopping mall, recreation park, tourist places, being introduced by friends and family members, and so forth. Finally, friendship is also created through unplanned situations like charity works, meeting on the street, at the bus stop, airport or train-station and many other unexpected occasions.

Knowing a basic system of interpersonal communication and relationship formation process is insufficient without further knowledge and skills to generate effective interaction. Notably, the psychological influence behind the route is the most important aspect that affects interpersonal communication and relationship creation. In particular, people need to understand the need to communicate; the important reasons to take into consideration in the process of relationship making; and the accuracy, usefulness, sufficiency, practicality and functionality of the ideas, intentions, message or information being communicated. Therefore, in order to improve the effectiveness of interpersonal relations and communication, people also need to comprehend forms of communication and manage the interaction process.

4 Forms of Communication

Basically, two forms of communication will be discussed in this chapter: verbal communication and non-verbal communication. Additionally, the authors believe that other forms of communication, such as business and intercultural communication, are vital and need extensive discussion. Selecting the appropriate form of communication is crucial to ensure that the transmitted or exchanged message is comprehensible. This will avoid possible interpersonal communication problems, misunderstanding, misinterpretation and conflict.

VERBAL INTERPERSONAL COMMUNICATION

Oral or verbal communication is an exchange of ideas, knowledge, intentions, feeling or perceptions that involves expression of voice or spoken words in order to transmit meaning (idea, intention or feeling). Verbal communication is a two-way communication found in face-to-face conversation, group discussion, telephone calls and other related circumstances. The main advantage of oral communication is that it promotes prompt feedback to identify the effectiveness or completeness of the message transmitted. The feedback comes in the form of verbal inquiry, agreement, facial expressions and body gestures. There are also some other unexpected effects obtained, such as tightening friendships, reducing cost and waiting time for responses, and increasing work productivity (quick action means work is done in a shorter time with prompt results).

However, inaccuracy of verbal communication occurs if the speaker chooses jargon or wrong words to convey the message or intention, or leaves out pertinent details. Some dangers or communication breakdown occur when the receiver misinterprets the meaning, forgets part or the entire message and/ or is disturbed by noises that will possibly disrupt the process. Hence, the effectiveness of oral communication depends on the quality or pitch of the voice and tone; speed of delivery; language, accent or dialect; body gesture, posture and distance from the receiver; and other health and hygienic factors (body odour, mouth smell, skin diseases, garment's cleanliness) the of communicator. Other aspects, such as reliability of communication media (minimal interruptions in the cellular network, walkie-talkie) and surrounding area (minimal noises) also play a role to ensure the verbal conversation is effective. Oral communication is often preferred when the message is personal, non-routine and brief. In addition, different words or phrases in a different language represent different meanings to the others. For example, 'chao' means 'go' in Chinese language but 'hello' in Vietnamese.

COMMUNICATION IN THE NETWORK AND WORK TEAMS

Communication in a group or a team can create an identical pattern to that featured in Figure 4.1. According to Lewis, Goodman and Fandt (2001), forming a group only incorporates people participation for certain purposes. Forming a team expecting people to participates and contributes towards goal accomplishment. There are five patterns of communication: a wheel, Y, chain, circle and all channels. Each communication pattern is formed according to the reasons for having a group or team, and intensity of interaction.

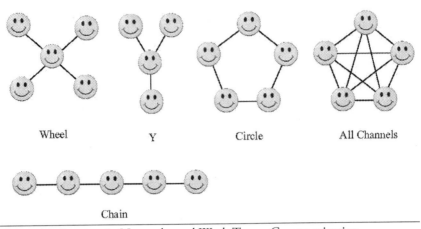

| Wheel | Y | Circle | All Channels |

Chain

Figure 4.1: Patterns in Networks and Work Teams Communication
Source: Lewis, Goodman and Fandt (2001)

1. The **Wheel** pattern shows the flow of communication activities are being controlled and monitored from a central point which is probably the group leader. In this centralized function, the leader receives information, creates the orders or instructions and is responsible for disseminating, delegating or assigning tasks to the other group members. For example, the company's Chief Executive Officer (CEO) is supported by his/her team members such as a Chief Operating Officer (COO), Chief Financial Officer (CFO), Chief Marketing Officer (CMO), Managing Director (MD) and other executives. The CEO is responsible for the whole organizational communication or project and other team members are in charge of the particular section or Small Business Unit (SBU). The leader might need complete information from all SBUs in order to make a critical decision, such as a new recruitment budget and so forth.

2. In the **Y** pattern, two or more people only interact with one person, who functions as a gate-keeper or a controller of the information. The gate-keeper or trustee represents a group and will interact and disseminate the information to the ground staff, subordinate or colleagues. This representative function is less centralized in decision making and functions merely as an information desk for the group. A main benefit from this pattern

of communication is a well organized information control or flow, managed by a person or committee which acts as a referee, source or secretariat for a program. However, the information controller may not be a favourable person to the group members or untrained, unskilled, inefficient or *ethnocentric* type of person.

3. A **circle** pattern of the communication path is where the information flows in closed circulation and the person who starts the communication will receive feedback from the last person who has received and responded to the message. This communication pattern is found in a group but probably not in a team. The information will go back to the source of the information after circulation among the group members in forms of feedback, amendment, agreement, additional information, correction or without any changes. Basically, information will circulate within the same department or position level, or be communicated to others according to their hierarchy, experience, function, purpose, beliefs, and area of expertise, location and interest. This one-to-one basis of interaction in a line probably involves different people with specific specialties or expertise, but linked-up for a single project. For example, to approve certain project, it requires a project manager, secretary, engineer, accountant, surveyor and architect to sign the paperwork for correction, amendment or approval. Each of the group members has the expertise to perform a specific task and ensure the accuracy of the information certification. However, the pace of information circulation could be slow or time consuming due to the parallelisation, hierarchy, level of competence or sense of urgency at every pit stop of group member's function, which passes over the information or documents one after another.

4. A **chain** pattern of communication is created when the information flows in a single line from one person to another. It is a one-to-one basis of interaction between two people along the *chain of command*. For example, for the procedures for job promotion or idea suggestions, a recommendation goes bottom-up, hierarchically by level for recruitment or appointment support and approval. Communication in chain pattern shows

a respect for the protocol in a *chain of command* and *line of authority* which will then guarantee information accuracy, security, support and recommendation. However, the information flows can be time consuming, delayed, expired or unachievable to the target, due to red tape, communication barriers or bias, personal interest, or misplaced and missing information.

5. The free flow of information circulating among all group members is known as **all channels** of communication pattern. It is the most decentralized flow of communication in which people team-up and interact more closely to discuss, change, comment, contribute or share information. In this type of communication pattern, every group members most probably participates equally, regardless of their background, job position or expertise. For example, all the family are invited to discuss the destination for a family trip, or holiday. This form of communication helps to generate various ideas from different perspectives, especially in problem-solving, closing a gap and creating a better relationship among group members, producing innovative and creative outcomes, and speeding up work accomplishment. However, in this communication pattern, there are tendencies to communication break-down such as: conflict of interest; ideas disagreement; misuse of power to get attention or approval in group work and activities; and assembling group members being time consuming and difficult.

Aligned with the discussion as above, the selection of appropriate communication channel or pattern depends on the background, position, function, hierarchy, distance and location of every group member, nature of the information, job or a task, and level of urgency for the information circulation.

ORGANIZATIONAL COMMUNICATION

In addition to communication in networks and work teams, there are two directions of information (vertical and horizontal) found in organizational interaction. In particular, organizational communications have different magnitudes of interaction effectiveness due to the existence of several layers of organisational hierarchy known as *chain of command.*

The relationships are represented by an organizational chart or structure, and every person has an exclusive work or job responsibility, academic background, expertise, power and authority. There are formal protocols that bridge the top-bottom or bottom-top relationship known as the *line of authority*. For example, there are the president at the top; executives, directors and managers in the middle; and supervisors, officers, clerks, office-boys, helpers, tea-ladies, telephonists and drivers at the bottom of the hierarchy.

1. In a **vertical** direction of communication, information flows up and down along the chain of command in the organizational structure. Usually, it goes along formal reporting lines which take place between managers and their subordinates. It might involve several different levels of the organization such as top managers, middle managers, front line managers, executives, supervisors and ground staff. The vertical direction of communication in the chain of command can go upward (bottom-up) or downward (top-bottom) communication.

   a. *Upward* communication carries the message from subordinates to superior or higher level of managers. The message comprises of work reports, suggestions, and corrections or complaints for the attention of top management members. The message typically involves official or unofficial messages related to the job, financial, sales performance or organizational activities. Other than writing report, memo or letters, a suggestion box is an example of upward communication tool to place responses, feedbacks, suggestions or complaints for the further attention or action of higher level personnel.

   b. In contrast, *downward* communication occurs when information flows down the hierarchy from higher level managers to subordinates. The message probably involves a new assignment, responsibility, authority, appointment, promotion, placement, and/or other feedback such as criticism, performance evaluation, acknowledgement, appreciation or suggestion. Sometimes, a short note or memo is issued directly or jumps across the organizational hierarchy for immediate notification of particular personnel, which requires a prompt response for urgent reaction and action. Furthermore, a notification or announcement could be placed on a notice board as a communication tool for general views.

2. A **horizontal** communication occurs when the message flows laterally across the formal chain of command, or across departments within the organization. It involves the sharing or circulating of information among colleagues and peers of the same interest, expertise, structure or hierarchical level in the organization. For example, a circular about the enforcement of the new standard requirement on performance appraisal' among senior lecturers. The purpose of this horizontal communication is to facilitate coordination among interdependent units. Sometimes, the organization breaks protocol in order to create rapport or build a harmonious working environment. Subordinates or different SBUs members can interact directly with top management or board of directors outside formal working hours or during social events or parties, family-day, company trips or holidays.

NON-VERBAL INTERPERSONAL COMMUNICATION

Non-verbal communication involves an exchange of the idea which does not require words to convey the message and carries meaning which is unable to be described through verbal communication. This form of communication is generated to acquire, develop or sustain interpersonal relations and interaction. The acceptance or effective communication circle depends on a person's point of understanding or frame of references to interpret the message or clues as conveyed by the sender. It often relies on written communication, which is represented by symbols to form a language to convey the message. Additionally, facial expression, body movements or gestures and physical contact are used in oral communication to put emphasis on the meaning.

1. **Written** communication is formed by transforming the idea into symbols, craft, writing, scratches, painting or drawings on a surface to convey a message. The message comes in various

forms such as memos, letters, reports, notes, painting, portraits, and other circumstances, in which words or symbols are arranged and used to transmit the meaning (ideas, intentions, feelings). Written communication can be a reasonably accurate medium which provides a permanent record for exchanges (such as a Memorandum of Understanding (MoU)), records or remembrances. For example, the Malaysian Declaration of Independence in 1957. Furthermore, the sender can tailor, draft or screen their message before transmitting it to the receiver. It enables communicators to transfer or share lengthy or complex ideas especially related to the scientific, technical or mechanical aspects, such as the electric and electronic circuit and blueprint of a building. In addition, written documents form main, additional or supporting materials for confirmation, interpretation and clarification of other forms of communication. Printed or written communication is important, especially in law, to avoid any consequences of misinterpretation or abuse of meaning (ideas, intentions, and feelings) of the messages. Accuracy of legal documentation (with stamping and attorney endorsement) is also used as solid affidavits (evidence) in court jurisdiction. Written communication is usually the best method to use when the message is more impersonal, routine, complex or longer.

However, the main drawback of using the written method is the time taken to prepare the documents. Furthermore, to ensure the documents are well written and precise requires particular knowledge and skill in language, grammar and formats. Preparation, proof-reading, editing or auditing must be carried out by persons empowered with particular authority. For example, a company's yearly financial reports must be prepared by a financial team including account clerks, account managers and accountants, endorsed by the Chief Financial Officer (CFO), audited by a registered audit firm, and approved by members of the Board of Directors and Secretary of the Company before being published for public view. Another example is that a blueprint of the building must be drawn and prepared by an architect and not by, for instance, a medical doctor.

Preparing written documents also involves financial cost for materials, equipment, design, editing, decorations, printing and binding. The written form of communication tends to be formal, and open to misinterpretation and misrepresentation of symbols. In some circumstances where communicators are situated in distant locations, written communication does not offer immediate feedback and tends to be exposed to danger such as loss or damage in transporting (conventional mail postage). Time factors often cause delay waiting for a response, during which information may become out-of-date, misused, or misplaced, and address become unreachable and so forth.

2. **Braille** writing is a special dot printing with special characters or symbols which represent certain meaning (ideas, intentions, and feelings) to form a message that helps blind people to obtain knowledge and communicate. It requires the tip of the fingers to touch the typing dots and to read and interpret a series of a messages and information. The main difficulty found in Braille writing is the need for a special device or dot printer to type the message. The typing machine and printed materials are also difficult to move around, and documents are costly and time consuming to prepare. In addition, special training is required to learn the dot symbols and operate the typing machine. However, in certain circumstances, Braille writing can be used to convey a private and confidential message. Only those who have knowledge of Braille writing can interpret the messages.

3. Apart from Braille writing, **sign** language is a medium of interaction, especially among deaf people, or people who having 'hard of hearing' or 'auditory challenged'. The meanings (ideas, intentions, and feelings) of words or phrases are shaped by the formation of fingers, hands, body or arm movement and facial expression. Figure 4.2 shows some samples of internationally accepted sign language. Similar to Braille writing, training is needed to learn the codes and form the messages to be able to communicate in sign language. It is time-consuming and requires extra effort and finance to buy a book or attend courses to learn the language. It should be noted that effective communication with sign language requires a face-to-face position and direct eye contact to read and understand the signing.

Figure 4.2: Sample of the Sign Language
http://www.cse.iitk.ac.in/users/se367/11/se367/ganuj/project/proposal.html (accessed on 2nd April 2014)

Importantly, Braille and sign language help disabled people to be part of the community, to interact, communicate and create relationships among each other and with others, especially those who are knowledgeable about the language.

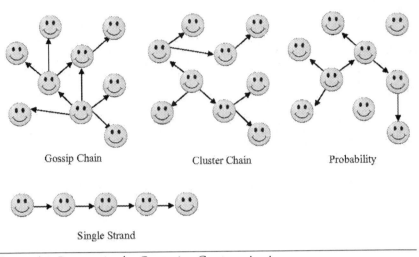

Gossip Chain   Cluster Chain   Probability

Single Strand

Figure 4.3: Patterns in the Grapevine Communication
Source: Lewis, Goodman and Fandt (2001)

4. In addition to organizational communication, the **grapevine** is an informal form of interaction. Figure 4.3 as above shows types of grapevines, which could be used to spread information within an organization.

    a. A *Gossip* chain occurs when a person spreads a message to many other people randomly. Each receiver in turn either keeps the information confidentially to him or herself or repeats the process to others. The policy maker can use the gossip method easily as it is an inexpensive method to get early feedback before launching a new project, or changing or enforcing new procedures. However, this method could harm the policy maker's personal image due to the false news, stories or propaganda which gossip often spreads around.

    b. In a *cluster* chain of communication, a person passes the information to a few people then directs the message to their own chain of command, or to close friends, sitting or working around their work-station. Perhaps, the message will eventually reach all the group members. The message could be similar or identical, such as new appointments, notification, acknowledgement or other common notices. The message could use oral or written forms of messages.

c. In a *single strand* form, the information spreads in a direct line or chain of communication on a one-to-one basis. The message could be slow during the process of passing from one person to another due to the level of confidentiality of the information. Only selected, favoured or close friends will receive the messages. This single strand form is similar to the chain pattern of formal communication.

d. In the *probability* form of grapevine, only a few identified, favoured, selected or related people will receive the information or messages. Once notified, some of the receivers will either direct messages to others or stop and keep it to themselves. Those who are not chosen or not able to receive the information are probably unreachable, unapproachable, do not belong to the interest group or might not be interested in the circulated message. For example, an invitation to a Quran recitation event is only directed to the Muslims in the organization.

5. **Body gestures** are forms of kinaesthetic reactions involving movements of any part of the body to convey a message about thought and emotion often reinforced with oral expression. A movement or a combination of arms, hands and facial expression might indicate a sign of boredom, interest, curiosity, excitement, acceptance, danger, rejection, annoyance, harassment. Other expressions can convey sadness, happiness, anger, disgust, fear, joy or surprise. In order to establish effective interpersonal relations and communication, it is important for a person to be aware of the usual or unusual gestures of the other person or group of people showing signals, responses or salient feedback. Therefore, it is crucial for a person or speaker to adjust their communication strategies, techniques and tactics to ensure that their message is reachable and understandable by the receiver. For example, a sign of "V" formed by two fingers is a symbol of victory or peace but reversed, is a very rude gesture in Britain!

Another example of the most common signal but with various possibility of interpretation is when a person crosses their arms across the chest. This usually indicates either an unconscious action; that they are deep in thought; or that they are silently expressing resistance or rejection.

6. **Body movement** is a motion of part of the whole body as a signal to support, emphasize or clarify the message (ideas, intentions or feelings) that is being verbally expressed. However, over emphasising or making too many movements could create distraction, insult or annoyance during a conversation, interaction or communication process. For example in public speaking, the spot you stand on stage, pace of movement and arm or hand motion are likely representing the personality, readiness or nerves of the speaker.

7. **Facial expression** is a motion using movement of the wrinkle lines and face muscles. It communicates information or indicates emotional expression or processes, and help to emphasize or reinforce oral expression, body gestures and movement. Appropriate facial expression moderates interpersonal behaviour and perception when expressing ideas. Common facial expressions reveal anger, disgust, fear, joy, sad or surprise. Studies (sees, Matsumoto, 2006; Mayer, DiPaolo & Salovey, 1990; Van Rooy & Viswesvaran; 2004) have found that emotional expression is related to a person's personality attributes. Additionally, such empirical studies have demonstrated biological and situational forces differentiate a character or personality from one person to another, especially in expressing emotions. In particular, it has been clinically proven that personality and emotion are often portrayed through facial mimic or expressions.

8. **Physical contact** is a visible reaction but invisible signal to convey a message of welcome, resistance, rejection, power, dominance, harassment and other emotions (anger, disgust, fear, joy, sadness or surprise). Physical contact has a different meaning across culture and personality background in social relations. Some examples of physical contacts are handshakes,

holding hands, back slapping or rubbing, kissing, hugging, patting the shoulder, arm brushing, pinching, striking, pushing, pulling, punching and kicking. Additionally, unconscious awareness about personal space also varies across culture groups. Interpersonal distance or space indicates the level of intimacy, respect, social status, ranking and stratification, especially within high-context cultures such as Malay, Indonesian, Thai and Japanese.

OTHER FORMS OF INTERPERSONAL COMMUNICATION

Effective and interactive communications are also important elements in business and intercultural contact. In general, business communication indicates flows of information within business networking or stakeholders (financial institutions, consumers, employees, industry, community, public, suppliers, manufacturers, warehouses, promoters, distributors, dealers, and retailers). Furthermore, intercultural communication is an interaction influenced by cultural elements, discussed later in this section.

Business Communication

A business is a commercial establishment to generate, transform, supply and trade the demand of products and/or services. Therefore, communication in business is vital to create an environment in which the entrepreneur or communicator initiates a commercial interaction and/or relations to fulfil the stakeholders' need and satisfaction on their investment return.

1. Basically, a business entity needs capital and financial support to set up while working capital sustains their operation. Establishing mutual *financial* communication is crucial to create and maintain investor and shareholder confidence. Mutually beneficial trust between a business and its investors and shareholders is critical as they are the source of capital for business (especially for company establishment with shares). Additionally, positive relationships are also important between a company and other financial communities such as banks, financial institutions, financial-related media and regulatory bodies.

2. ***The Consumer*** is an individual, group of people or organizations who use business products or services. Maintaining good communications with customers is vital as they define the financial return and sustainability of a business. Types of customers include the end-customers (consuming products or using services themselves) or industrial customers (purchasing products or using services to produce other forms of commercial products or services). Thus, selecting the most appropriate and cost-efficient marketing strategies is important in order to gain the attention of new customers, retain current customers or persuade former customers to resume their purchasing. Therefore, appropriate budgeting and selection of marketing strategies and business media (such as advertisement in television channels, radio, magazine, website, billboard, flyers or messaging through cellular phone) are necessary to establish effective business communication with customers.

3. Other important business relations are communication with ***employees***. Employees are considered a part of the business community or stakeholders as they contribute directly or indirectly to the daily commercial operations. The workforce is the main drive to support business owner in reaching the ultimate goal: *economies of scale* (reducing production costs, increasing or maintaining the quality of the products or services and profit maximization). Furthermore, with their knowledge, skills, expertise or specialties, the workforce will help to ensure resource efficiency and the effectiveness of business decisions. Hence, in order to develop co-operative relationships with employees, a business entity needs to acknowledge or appreciate employees' contributions by reward giving, providing appropriate welfare, and including employees' family members (for example: with gifts for a new born baby, or reward for excellent academic achievements). In addition, Occupational Safety and Health (OSH) are critical issues of concern to the business, to ensure workers are working in a safe and healthy workplace. Ignorance of OSH requirements will incur additional or unexpected costs to the business. Costs to OSH non-compliance include insurance or compensation to the workers who are involved in accidents

(leading to hospitalisation, injury or death) which happen in the workplace during working hours due, for instance, to insufficient safety precautions or non-ergonomic machines and equipment.

4. ***Industrial relations*** establish a union, association or business amalgamation to promote fair competition among businesses and to support each other. For example, the establishments such as Malaysian Franchise Association, Association of Banks in Malaysia, and National Association of Women Entrepreneurs of Malaysia (NAWEM) have the main purpose of supporting business expansion, protecting members and advising on possible business fraud.

5. The general society or public ***community's*** involvement seems to be indirectly contributing to the business well-being. A community is probably a group of people or an organization that do not purchase, use or consume the organization's products or services. However, they are probably living, working or operating, around the business entity. The community members have the right to place complaints to the particular legal authority in regard to any business fraud, ignorance, or environmental issues caused by the company. Community legal action against the business entity may incur additional costs to the company, such as paying authority or a court summons, compensation for damages made, operational shut-down or image damage. Therefore, it is valuable for business entities to have a corporate social responsibility (CSR) plan and activities to build beneficial rapport with the public society or community. Some examples of CSR activities are: environmental concern and declarations, charitable work, donations, sponsorships and social works.

6. Business entities should plan good communications, with statutory and governmental agencies as their priorities. Mutual ***public*** relations are essential to ensure the businesses follow and fulfil the business operational requirement according to the statutory law, rules and regulations. However, it is important to ensure the business does not commit illegal activities such as

smuggling, bribery, corruption, insider trading or other public disservices.

7. Beneficial communications and relations with **other entities or stakeholders** in business networking such as: suppliers, manufacturers, warehouses, promoters, distributors, dealers, and retailers, also contribute to the success of the business. A business may approach each line member with different communication approaches and strategies, based on their relationship goals and outcomes to the business.

Intercultural Communication

Culture is a sum of values, beliefs, rules, norms, techniques, institutions and artefacts that represent image or identity of a human population. Culture is defined as a "collective mental programming or a system of collectively held values, shared with other members and used  to distinguish the members from other groups" (Hofstede, 1983: p.76). Culture consists of learned behaviour passed down through generations, which shows a unique identity or lifestyle of a particular group or society. The elements of a culture include learned characteristics and interrelated cultural components and are shared among the group members, hence defining the boundaries of the group. The components of the culture include: aesthetics, attitudes and beliefs, religion, material possessions, education, language, societal organization, legal characteristics and political structures. Therefore, different cultural groups have identical components which vary in character from one to another. In addition, culture is part of human attributes that affect their norms, habits, perceptions, emotional expression and other basic rules of life which are known as cultural *frames of references* (Torbiorn, 1982).

Communicating with people with different cultural frames of reference may either create possible excitement or confusion, especially to the sojourner. According to Ward, Bochner and Furnham (2001), sojourners are defined as individuals or groups of people such as expatriates, international students, travellers, tourists, immigrants and asylum seekers, who travel outside their own home country. Intercultural conflict, difficulty, anxiety or uncertainty occurs due to dissimilar perspectives of appropriate and inappropriate interpersonal understanding and behaviour (Ali, Van der Zee & Sanders, 2003; Gudykunst, 1997, 2005; Martinko & Douglas, 1999; Nishida, 1999; Searle & Ward, 1990; Selmer, 2007; Selmer & Lauring, 2009; Torbiorn, 1982; Ward, Bochner & Furnham, 2001). According to Ting-Toomey and Takai (2010), intercultural conflicts take place when visible or invisible elements of culture are in conflict due to incompatibility of cultural backgrounds, understandings, expectations, views, values, norms, beliefs, orientations or power. A conflict exists when a person feels emotionally threatened and becomes a barrier to the interaction process that jeopardizes the completeness and effectiveness of communication.

Having sufficient cultural knowledge and skills is important especially when encounter cultural differences abroad. Interpersonal communication and relationship signals could intrepretes differently from a culture to another. For example, nodding the head indicates a receiver agrees about something in most cultural groups, but a sign of understanding (but not yet agreeing) or showing respect in Japan. Therefore, according to the Anxiety/Uncertainty Management (AUM) theory, strangers could take charge, gain advantage and practice communication effectiveness through appropriate "mindful management of anxiety and uncertainty levels of interactions" (Gudykunst, 2005).

Cultural stratification or categorization indicates different procedures, intentions and direction of communication. According to Hall (1959), people from high context cultures such as Malaysia, Indonesia, China and Japan find indirect ways to communicate and incorporate implicit influence of personal or physical context in communication. For example, the concepts of the *face* and *guanxi* in Chinese culture specify a value of communication network or relations (Friedman, 2009). In contrast, explicit influence leads to language or distinct communication where relations were found among low context cultures such as Americans, Canadians, and Germans.

The assimilation of sojourners into different groups or cultural environments and association by inter-cultural marriage or adoption creates intercultural relations and integration. Intercultural difficulties could affect psychological and socio-cultural well-being and fitness, especially in interpersonal and group communication and relations. Different languages, spoken or written, are the most obvious source of intercultural communication difficulty. People from different cultural groups may speak in different languages or dialects, using different accents, word formations, vocabulary and semantics, and different interpretations of the meanings (ideas, perceptions or feelings). In addition, sojourners or strangers with insufficient information or understanding of host nationals' cultural background may cause further misunderstanding or misinterpretation of cultural behaviour. This scenario is known as cultural blunder: for example, some Americans failed to sell 29-inch tables in Japan (where the average table height is 20 inches) as Japanese sit on the floor at the table and they do not use chairs, due to their tradition and small spaces in Japanese homes.

Scholars including Black, Mendenhall & Oddou, 1991; Brewster & Scullion, 1997; Caligiuri, 1997; Claus & Briscoe, 2009; Forster, 1997; Harzing, 1995; Mendenhall, Stevans, Bird & Oddou, 2008 affirmed that ineffective intercultural understanding creates misleading marketing messages, incapable and incompetent expatriates, and international assignment difficulties and failures. This also creates unawareness of the local business environment, an ineffective supply chain and local support, and other communication breakdowns. A few examples of expatriates' failures and difficulties include the incapability to accomplish international assignments, to establish assignment goals, incomplete international missions and early return.

Therefore, it is essential to acquire sufficient cultural knowledge about the target destination before committing to international mobility. There are many sources to obtain cultural knowledge, either through training or reading material from the internet, books, travel magazines, embassies and other travel agencies. Sufficient cultural knowledge will help sojourners to avoid cultural difficulties, confrontation or psychological and socio-cultural uncertainty, which results in a feeling of isolation, annoyance, being ignored or unwelcome in culturally strange place.

5 Forms of Relationship

As discussed in Chapter Two, a relationship is defined as a human connectedness, chemistry or networking. Relationships are established and developed for reasons. People may have different feelings, intentions and perceptions in the relationship building. The intensity of the relationships also depend on the goals, knowledge, skills, socio-cultural influences (such as values, norms, beliefs), attitudes, perceptions, status, and other emotional and psychological preferences. There are various types of relationships established formally or informally, by planning or coincidence, through searching or arranged introductions, with imagined or actual physical contact and so forth. Types of relationship will be discussed in the following sections.

ROMANTIC RELATIONSHIP

A romantic relationship is established with affective response, such as feeling and emotion that will give a sensual impact such as love, pity, intimacy, and other companionship responses. The differences in the romantic responses depend on people's knowledge, goals, preferences, experiences, appearance, personality or other socio-cultural influences. For example, some people perceive a man with a rough voice or a woman with a soft voice as romantic. In particular, an emotional affiliation will establish closeness of interpersonal interaction, conversation, participation and involvement, with some intention to establish a certain degree of relationship. A romantic relationship anticipates a degree of trust, passion, commitment, response and involvement to ensure beneficial outcomes and maintain the rapport for lasting connectedness. A mutual romantic relationship requires a similar intentions, feelings and perception of responses from the other. The existence of a romantic relationship enables people to share and exchange feelings, perceptions, emotions, thoughts, beliefs, stories, knowledge, experiences, information and secrets. According to DeVito (2009) there are six types of romantic relationship of love: eros, ludus, storge, pragma, mania and agape as shown in the Figure 5.1. Each of these relationship types will create a degree of closeness or complexity.

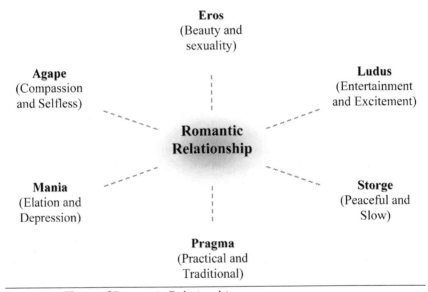

Figure 5.1: Types of Romantic Relationship

1. **Eros**. Looks, appearance, cleanliness, image, beauty, physical shape are a major focus in this romantic relationship. A sensual response, imagination, feelings, perceptions and attractiveness stimulates willingness and desire to establish intimate interpersonal relations and communication. An erotic person is concerned with and sensitive to criticism and physical imperfections, protocol, etiquette and image especially when with partner, spouse, colleagues and in public.

2. **Ludus**. A romantic relation is created by the ludus type of person only for companionship, in order to avoid loneliness, discrimination by others on the masculinity or femininity image. Love or intimate relations are not taken too seriously. They will retain the partner as long the partner is interesting and amusing.

3. **Storge**. A relationship created by the storge type of person lacks passion and intensity. The relationship is established for companionship for certain goals or purposes. The relationship may dissolve once their needs and wants are fulfilled or satisfied. A storge lover is selective in choosing a partner, and the relationship is created only with those whom they know and can share an interest with.

4. **Pragma**. The relationship established by pragma lover is based on real reasons, logic and preferred background. The relationship is created with a compatible partner who fulfils their important needs, wants and desires. For example, a relationship with a millionaire's daughter, with the aim of getting a business contract.

5. **Mania**. A mania relationship is characterised by extreme high or low connections or impacts. The romantic or intimate relationship may create extremely jealousy or obsessive effects, depending on the intensity or changes of the relationship.

6. **Agape**. An imaginary or spiritual love is created with unconditional expectations although there are no close ties or intimate relations with the subject. Agape relations are not established with concern to gain personal benefit, but for psychological and emotional satisfaction. In certain circumstances, the agape, believer or religious follower may create a danger to others with their extreme conviction of the existence of spiritual power, influence, or taboo.

Additionally, a certain degree of courtesy, effort, commitment and passion are required to obtain benefits from the romantic relationship. Compromising, "give-and-take", negotiating, understanding and communicating are the basis of maintaining the romantic chemistry among couples. In circumstances of interpersonal conflict, keeping silent or a temporary separation is a solution to re-build trust and respect, and reduce uncertainty and tension. Hence, different communication skills are required for different types of romantic relationship (with spouse, children, partner, family, relatives, subordinate/superior and society). The romantic skills involve a quantity and quality of voice and intonation (rough, firm, soft, paused, static or melodious); language used (words, phrases, sentences, grammar, messages, meanings, dialects or slang); and physical contact (prolonged eye contact, touches, facial expression, and body movements and distance). A symbolic communication such as gift giving, surprises or certain salient behaviours (such as offered help, advice, guidance or belongings) are able to convey a romantic signal of love, respect, trust, acceptance, sympathy, appreciation or acknowledgement.

Effective romantic relationships are also guided or influenced by socio-cultural factors such as religion, ethnicity, race, gender, status, ranking or hierarchy. For example, Muslims are forbidden to have an intimate relationship with the other gender (man and woman) without by-marriage relations. In addition, in individualistic or low-context cultures, the term 'romantic relationship' refers to love, dating or sexual intimacy and individual fulfilment. In contrast, in collective or high-context cultures, romantic relationships are more spread into a larger social scope of connections, networks, or people's relatedness. However, incompatible feedback, hidden information, secret affairs, inappropriate approaches or force in romantic relationships cause rejection, annoyance and denial. Ignorance will destroy trust, respect and intimacy, and may create social problems such as exploitation, discrimination, bias, harassment, rape, arguments or fights.

FAMILY RELATIONSHIP

The family is a social unit in which people are together with a certain magnitude or intensity of relatedness, connection, networking and relationship. Most of the time, members of the family are engaged in informal communication, sharing stories, problems, activities, success, achievement, happiness or sadness. A certain degree of self-disclosure, trust and respect is given or received, varied according to the age, status, ranking, hierarchy and distance within families. In the Asian high-context culture, the family unit is given a priority, especially among

Malays, who maintain togetherness among family members possibly to the death. However, closeness within families gives some social difficulties or problems (such as accusations of cronyism, nepotism, corruption or bias) when involving public image, and large scale businesses, and political affairs.

The communication pattern, direction and intensity also varies depending on biological or demographical aspects (such as age, gender), status, ranking and hierarchy within families. Three forms of familial communication include equality, compatibility and fragility. First, the communication is considered **equal** when the communicators have a similar level of ability, credibility, knowledge and skills on certain issues. Openness and honesty establish equality of communication. Equality is easily obtained, especially among communicators of the same gender. In addition, equality in the familial relationship enables the information to be shared and direct (straight to the point) within the interpersonal discussion or conversation. A leisure type of relationship foresees interpersonal conflict as solvable and not threatening. Secondly, **compatible** communication is created when people are interdependent with similar or balanced physical, psychological and emotional strength and capability. Each person has the authority and specialty in certain areas of knowledge or expertise. For example, a couple is helping each other when the wife has a passion for child care while the husband has an interest or capability in cooking. Equality to the amount of effort given is important to maintain the relationship, and interpersonal conflicts are non-threatening.

Third, **fragile** communication occurs when one person dominates the relationship. A person may use power, authority, status, knowledge, skills or expertise to influence or control the situation, decision or communication. Exploitation, bias or discrimination may happen in the relationship in order to obtain trust, obedience, loyalty or respect. Interpersonal conflict occurs when the less attractive, powerless or discriminated partner takes revenge or challenges the relationship. Lastly, the influence of power, social status, ranking, hierarchy or egos will create a **strained** communication with imbalanced responses or outcomes. A one-way communication is created in forced communication, in which the messages are conveyed by a person with authority who uses power, image, status or ranking to control or dominate the interactions or conversations session.

Characteristic of the Family

As mentioned earlier, a family is a unit in which people share ideas, philosophy, interests, values, norms or beliefs. Familial relationship is established by kinship, referral or marriage. Thus, there are some definite characteristic of a family relationships, including:

1. *Roles.* In particular, each person within a family has a defined role (such as cook, child-carer or wealth earner) based on their mutual understanding. A harmonious family needs to have equal responsibility to ensure the daily housework (such as laundry, cooking and cleaning) is shared and conducted together. A traditional form of the family has divided roles: the man as main wage earner and wife as housekeeper. This situation may create tension especially for a 'career' wife with a double burden (responsibility in the office and at home). Thus, in modern life where both husband and wife are working, some people choose to hire a fulltime live-in housemaid to take care of daily housework.

2. *Responsibility.* To ensure mutual understanding and effective familial relationships, every family member has particular obligations, contributions, roles, authority and responsibilities. For example, responsibilities from the perspective of time, promises, financial, emotional, physical, societal and social relations.

3. *Shared.* Most of the values, norms and beliefs are shared among the family members. Shared values are important to develop mutual and beneficial relationships in which family members understand and respect each other. However, not all information, events, wealth and stories are shared between family members for reasons that are individual and personal, or sentimental. In certain circumstances, family matters are shared or disclosed to the public when one or more family members are celebrities, ministers or other public figures. Publically sharing family matters could help to show social integrity, trust and respect, and hence avoid gossip, misinterpretation, and other social ills (such as bribery, corruption and nepotism).

4. ***Formation***. Many factors create the direction, effectiveness and stability of the family relationship. Career and other social obligations (such as job, ranking, status, hierarchy and other community services) determine a harmonious and stable family. Although a family shares living space and wealth; due to career needs, some couples and their family members are forced to live separately and have a long-distance relationship. Thus, understanding, trust and respect are vital to ensure an effective and lasting relationship. However, recent communication technology such as internet, Skype, messenger, video call, twitter and other chatting mediums help to maintain long-distance relationships.

Types of the Family

Numbers, intensity or magnitude of relationship among people or members of the group determines the form and size of the family. A family may be established through kinship (connections by blood), adoption, referral, arrangement; or be created for certain reasons, purposes or events.

1. ***Immediate Family***. A traditional form of the family is a social unit including a father, mother and children. Normally, the family members are interdependent and share a common system of values, norms, beliefs and philosophy of life. A beneficial relationship is established with mutual cooperation, understanding, sacrifices and compromises among members of the family unit. An immediate family also refers to a newly-wed couple, couple without children or single parents (unmarried, widowed, separated or divorced). Culture may also influence the establishment and preservation of the family. For example, in Western countries, children are expected to be independent and live their own life when they reach age eighteen. However, in high-context cultures like Malaysia especially among Malays, family connection is a priority, preferring a large number of families living together.

2. ***Extended Family***. A family unit refers to kinship connection by marriage or adoption. An extended family refers to the family

expansion which comprises grandfather/grandmother, father/mother, children (son/daughter), siblings (brother/sister), uncle/aunt, cousin/nephew, and grandson/granddaughter. In Malaysia, especially among Malays, closeness of family relations could reach the third layer (such as second or third uncle/aunt, cousin/nephew) of the family tree. In certain circumstances, it is a pride to gather the connectivity of family extension to many layers or generations of the family tree, and establish an official 'family club'.

3. ***Attached family.*** A family unit refers to the people who are connected to each other without kinship or marriage. These couples are engaged, dating, or living together (without legally being married), seeing the relationship as a matter of convenience, security, shelter, life partnership or companionship. Those people have little desire or are not yet ready to be united as a marriage couple in a family unit. They might be in a process of evaluating each other, considering any consequences after being married or winning family support or trust to accept a new member into the existing family unit. Each person might have separate, identical or exclusive psychological and physical space, values, norms, beliefs and perspectives of life. Some issues to take into account in establishing a family unit include expenditure, responsibilities, obligations, personal space, other social relationships, interpersonal crisis or conflict, and cost of divorce or death.

4. ***Shared Family.*** There are social units, couples or groups of people being together or connected to each other without a kinship of legal marriage relationship. Those people are connected due to similarity of interest, destiny, goal, project, activities and geographical or distance factors. This shared family can be found in shelter houses, associations, institutions, clubs, housing estates, villages and particular locations. For example, the Malaysia-Wellington Postgraduate Students Association assembles the students studying in Wellington, New Zealand and their family members for activities and support as a family. Such social support is important as they are away from home,

outside their cultural comfort zone and also for security reasons. The relationship and connectivity could last forever, be temporary while living and studying abroad, or dissolve once goals are accomplished or achieved.

Family Circle

Life is a cycle. The authors foresee a circle of family's establishment as shown in the figure 5.2. Upon maturity (general acceptance for definition of young adult is age eighteen), a man or a woman is allowed to be legally married and start his/her own family unit. A *single* person may be looking for a partner on their own initiative, or may be referred or introduced by family members, friends, colleagues; or through the Internet's social networking (such as Facebook, twitter, or blog). The personality, family, academic level, financial status and other factors are assessed and evaluated to determine a potential suitable match. Finding a suitable partner is important to establish mutual rapport, understanding, love, trust and respect, and to ensure both (man and woman) can live together and share familial matters for the rest of their lives. It rare for modern family unit to be established through arranged marriage by and among the family members.

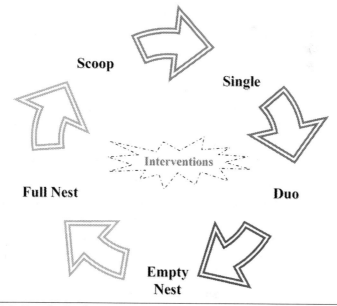

Figure 5.2: Family Circle

Once personal references are matched, and a suitable candidate has been met, a couple will start dating and create a *duo* family. Further personality and physical traits, as well as demographic background, will be observed and evaluated. A duo may be dating at a distance (a long-distance relationship) due to career and other social and geographical influences. Dating at distance makes it harder to establish understanding, trust, respect, integrity, responsibility, loyalty and honesty. It is also more difficult to establish the partner's beliefs, intentions, feelings and perception. There are many elements put into consideration in a process of establishing a serious relationship. These include members of family, friends and society, financial and economic costs and benefits, level of intelligence, and religious and other cultural elements (values, norms, and beliefs).

Next, some couples may unite and sustain the relationship by becoming legally married, living together, or being attached just for life partnership or companionship. An establishment of a united family unit with chosen 'soulmate' is labeled as an *empty nest.* An empty nest refers to a newly married couples without children (either planned or due to medical and health difficulties), or a married couple with a distance-relationship living separately due to job requirements, assignment, training and studying.

Once a couple has children a family unit is labeled as a *full nest* family. Basically, a full nest comprises father/mother and son(s)/daughter(s). As mentioned earlier, each family member plays particular roles, such as a wage earner, housekeeping, helper and such. A family member has a responsibility to give commitment, respect, trust and understanding in order to sustain the established family unit. Additionally, a full nest could include other family members such as in-laws (father/mother, brother/sister), grandfather/grandmother, uncle/aunt, cousin/nephew and adopted children.

When the family unit naturally dissolved by death or divorce, it is referred to as a *scoop*. Apart from death, the existence of a third party into family life (having affairs) or other social influences creates problems, conflicts or crisis which may force a family to separate or divorce. At these times, appropriate interpersonal communication is vital to ensure sustainability of the family unit. Apart from death or separation, some of the family members are naturally separated as the children reach the age at which they establish their own family's life cycle. Hence, the circle continues until a person may revolve back to a *single* life due to the job or family forces, separation, divorce or death.

FRIENDSHIP RELATIONSHIP

According to Schutz (1991, 2005) in his Theory of Interpersonal Needs, people need the presence of others for emotional, psychological or physical support and protection. In particular, friendship is created to fulfil certain needs such as: utility (to use the skills of the other); affirmation (to gain recognition, acknowledgement or notification); ego-support (to convince or persuade); stimulation (to create new ideas, suggestions, innovations or creations); and security (to protect from danger, exploitation, or threat).

Two or more independent people who can get along share the similarities in faith, values, norms, interests, perceptions and feeling which establish the level of friendship. However, the closeness of friendship is dependent on the intensity of the friendship goal. People are looking for the other with the intention to create an intimate relationship, or companionship, or partnership. A friendship may start when a person attends an event or participates in activities or at the workplace with colleagues, or between neighbours or school-mates. Referred friendship could also happen when a person is introduced to the other by friends or self-searched through social networks (such as pen-pals, facebook, twitter, or blogger). Most important of all the above, the key to sustain a mutual friendship is to be trustworthy, have a positive attitude and behave with respect and understanding. According to DeVito (2009), three types of friendship are:

1. **Reciprocity.** This is an ideal relationship where connectedness is created with a balance of giving and taking. The connectedness among people is created through respect, understanding, loyalty, sacrifice, affection and generosity. The goal of a reciprocity friendship is equality in shared activities, values and expected outcomes.

2. An imbalance of giving and taking between two or more people will create a **receptivity** friendship. Only one or few people within a group contribute and the rest (probably with less power or lower social status) act as listeners or followers. People who

have power will dominate the friendship in setting the goals, actions, activities and decisions.

3. A cordial but less intense friendship is known as **association**. Connectivity or togetherness among people is created for a particular goal, mission, activity or event. For example the Boy-Scouts, or Malays Association. An association is established to assemble people who share similar interests, expertise, knowledge, skills, faith, opinions or social needs.

Sustainability of friendship is dependent on the benefits gained from the establishment of connectivity, networking or relatedness. Continuity of the relationship depends on the need fulfilment of personal goals, impersonal, interpersonal, psychological and physical communication and relations. Hence, the establishment of mutual friendship goes through three stages, starting from contact, followed by involvement and finally an intimate relationship. First, people search for somebody to connect by creating a **contact**. People in contact may come from the local area; may be colleagues or school friends; attending same courses, events or activities; could share similar interests; or contact may be based on their appearance, personality, status or hierarchy. At this initial stage, people may openly propose a connection without intention to have close relations. The others' demographic background (such as age, interest, family, academic level, and career) are assessed to identify chemistry (possibility of connection). Once a match is met, a person will create a rapport by starting certain types of *involvement*. People will start to participate in the activities in order to have clear views of politeness, trust, understanding and other costs and benefits of the relationship. A beneficial relationship is obtained through dyadic consciousness, sense of togetherness and positive attitude emerges.

The confidence to connect with someone is created once the character meets the preferences (regarding personality, image, needs and goals) or is given encouragement to have a close and **intimate** friendship. A person foresees himself/herself or the other as an exclusive companion that is compatible. Uncertainty or doubt about the other will reduced, and trust and loyalty will be increased when people start to share and exchange stories and are together for activities. At the point of intimate relationship, people are able to predict the other's behaviour and read their nonverbal signs with accuracy, confidence and trust.

However, culture plays a role in establishing beneficial friendships which are guided by certain norms, values and beliefs. Educational level, race, religion, ethnicity, place of origin, and socio-economical aspects all determine the protocol, status, hierarchy, level and intensity of friendship establishment. For example, in Muslim societies, men and women not legally married or not having kinship relations are prohibited to have an intimate relationship. In addition, personal space and distance is psychologically enforced in creating relationships among Western cultures. Body language and other nonverbal signs are observed to avoid harassment, exploitation and other dangers.

WORKPLACE RELATIONSHIP

Companionships with beneficial relationships are also needed at the workplace, especially to ensure group or team work effectiveness. Although formal relationships at the workplace are created through an assigned 'chain of command' or 'line of authority', informal relationships are needed to obtain support and create a harmonious working environment. However, every organization may have an identical organizational culture that determines the direction and intensity of formal and informal relationships. There is an exclusive organizational culture that has been created to represent the corporate image and differentiate from other organizations or workplaces. The organizational culture is based on corporate identity, values, norms and beliefs which are guided by the organizational corporate goals, mission and vision. Assigned job responsibility, power and authority form a **formal relationship** established through the organizational structure. The relationship between superior-subordinates or employer-employees is shown through the line of authority. The designation indicates the relationship boundaries, ranking, status and hierarchy in the organization. There are certain protocols that determine interpersonal relationships and the direction of communication among organizational members.

Mentoring is an interpersonal relationship established dependant on the seniority (senior-junior) of the people at the workplace. A senior officer or executive will guide, explain or demonstrate the job to a newly recruited staff member. In addition, an experienced person with particular knowledge, information or skills will help to train others in the proper way of doing things. Mentoring might exist in an indirect or informal way: either assigning the job or completing a formal form during the off-the-job, or in-service training, face-to-face or online or in writing. Besides, in a process of restructuring the organizational structure, or changes in policy or operating procedures, superiors will update and mentor subordinates by updating them.

For business entities, **networking** relationships or other stakeholders is important to ensure sustainability, supply chain strengthening, market expansion and growth of the organizations. As discussed in Chapter Three, networking with stakeholders includes the customers, suppliers, manufacturers, financial institutions, society and government. At individual levels, a person may create a personal network within the organization or with others from different organizations, to obtain support, power and influence, or exchange or share information, knowledge and skills. Individual networking may be established in at formal or informal occasion with people he/she already known, referred or introduced by others, contact made by others, or strangers.

Lastly, a **romantic** relationship may be established in the workplace which indicates closeness of relations among members of the organization, department or unit. A romantic relationship does not necessarily indicate intimate or sexual relations, but merely showing respect, harmonious and familial forms of the relationship. In the Asian high-context culture, social status, hierarchy and age automatically has a significant influence on the relationships between elders and youngsters. However, although superior or much older than the subordinate, in certain circumstances, the boss or employer may greet the subordinate with social greeting such as '*pakcik*' (uncle), '*abang*' (brother) or '*kakak*' (sister). However, it is a challenge to people with kinship relations or couples likes husband-wife or dating couples working in the same place but of different rank, status or designations. Thus, professionalism is important to determine the workplace relationship to avoid bias, tension, nepotism, cronyism and negative gossip from others.

OTHER TYPES OF RELATIONSHIP

As mentioned in Chapter Three, there are certain obligations to the **public or society** with the existence or wealth of the organization in a place. This public or societal obligation is known as corporate social responsibility. Although the public or society does not connect directly with the organization, public involvement and acknowledgement is important to keep a good image, and maintain support and positive comments especially pertaining to environmental concerns.

Higher levels of relationship which require higher authority involvement are known as **governmental** relationships. A Governmental (government-to-government or G2G) relationship is established through proper diplomatic relations by the head of the country with the other nation to maintain national and regional security, sovereignty protection and socio-economic development. However, whether a beneficial G2G relationship is obtained depends on the country's political ideology and stability. Recent issues of terrorism and economic attack show the need for regional support and cooperation among nations.

There are relationships created which are considered as abnormal or unusual behaviour known as **supernatural** relationship. A supernatural relationship is created with non-human creators (such as a genie and Satan) when some magical power is needed for protection or healing purposes. People may also use the supernatural power to obtain respect, support and wonder from others. This may involve voodoo, taboo, Animism (a belief in the impersonal power behind material or objects) or unusual offerings, spells or practices.

Moving on, an **imaginary** relationship is established through religious or spiritual belief and faith in a God. Judaism, Christianity and Islam are the Monotheistic religions of God, revealed through the divine revelations of holy books, prophets and messengers. There is spiritual philosophical teaching such as Hinduism, Buddhism, Jainism and Sikhism which believe that the relationship with the universe is achieved through incarnations of the Holy Spirit in objects. Besides, those beliefs are based on the spiritual Guru's teaching on appropriate human good manners and behaviour. There are faiths that believe in an objects' spirit such as Japanese's Shinto, Chinese's Feng Shui, Naturalism and other tribal Animism beliefs. In addition, there are individuals who are known as free-thinkers, atheists and agnostics who do not believe in the existence of God. Their faith is guided by the flows of life, daily consequences, forces of nature and dependence on human-to-human relationships.

Finally, there is a difference between spiritual and religious stances. In general, a spiritual person refers to the association with a private realm of thought and experiences through meditation and revitalization. On the other hand, religiosity is created through connectivity with the public realm of membership and participation in particular religious teachings, institutions, rituals, worshipping and denominational doctrines, ideology, principles and philosophy.

ISSUES IN THE RELATIONSHIP

Distrust, betrayal, rebellion and back-stabbing are some negative effects of violence in relationships. Relationship violence occurs due to: misunderstanding, unjust treatment or one-sided benefits, or is influenced by the negative gossip of third parties. Relationship violence manifests itself either in verbal, emotional or physical harassment, abuse, annoyance, denial or exploitation. The effects of relationship violence may create emotional, physical, psychological or sexual abuse as well as injuries, social problems, and even death. The violence happens when a person's will experience:

- Constant insults, denial, annoying or ignorant behaviour.
- Restrictions to job promotions, spending, work space socio-cultural distance.
- Jealousy without acceptable reasons.
- Sexist harassment and behaviour, verbal or nonverbal.
- All communication ending in a quarrel and anger.

To avoid, deal with or solve relationship violence, a victim needs to be rational and invite the instigator to have a diplomatic and professional discussion to find possible solutions to the crisis. Sometimes, the use of third parties such as higher authorities or counsellors is deemed applicable in bridging the conflict.

6 Emotions in Communication and Relationship

Emotion is an affective reaction to the responses received or given. Emotion is a form of feelings reacting to the perception and expectation of needs and wants fulfilment. In interpersonal relations and communication, emotion plays a role that portrays the behaviour and personality of a person. Specifically, emotion takes place to communicate feelings by verbal or nonverbal reactions. The ability to manage and suppress emotions appropriately is known as emotion intelligence, which will be discussed in the following section.

PRINCIPLES OF EMOTIONS

As mentioned, emotion is a medium to communicate feelings that convey messages that are probably unable to be spoken or written. Ineffective communication occurs when a person misinterprets or fails to read the emotional clues of the others. For example, a baby's cry is probably because he/she has a stomach-ache but is not thirsty or hungry. There are several principles that form emotions:

1. **Basic reaction**. There are basic responses that portray the affective reaction of emotions, including joy, fear, surprise, anger, disgust and sadness. These basic reactions show a signal of acceptance, rejection or anticipation. Hence, effective

interpersonal communication and relationship is established when a person (receiver) is able to interpret the emotional meaning of the sender. Additionally, there are blended emotions where several characteristics of emotions are combined to reinforce the meaning. For example, love is created by the combination of joy and surprise; fear and elation on the Fairground rides.

2. **Body, mind and soul**. Emotions are depicted through particular body reactions especially gestures, movement and facial expressions. For example, people will look down to the floor whenever being humiliated or embarrassed and feel angry if someone being rude. In addition, a 'stage-fright' such as hands shaking or sweating palms happens when people are nervous, especially when giving a speech in front of strange audiences. Additionally, a personal inner force of soul created through culture (beliefs, norms and values) also has a significant influence on emotional reactions. Culture guides a person to make appropriate responses to interpret and express the emotions. For example, Westerner prefers to speak or behaviourally shows emotion but Asians are quieter whenever encountering a mismatch of feelings, perceptions, opinions or expectations.

3. **Adaptation**. It is vital for a person to adjust their emotions when encountering interpersonal conflict, crisis or difficulties. When coming into a new cultural environment, some behaviour could be perceived as inappropriate, rude, annoying or disgusting. Cultural sensitivity, and awareness of the other's socio-cultural background, rather than making quick assumptions, is important to avoid misunderstanding, misinterpretation and miscommunication. Conversely, inability to regulate the emotion or make necessary adaptation will affect the emotional state. Hostile feelings, disorientation or isolation is a consequence of not adapting to the environmental changes. Hence, a person needs to realize the need to accept and respect differences and suppress their emotion appropriately.

4. **Communication**. A person is supposed to have the power to control their emotions. The cognitive strength (mental

interpretation and judgement to the responses) influence the affective responses (feelings) which lead to behaviour and expression. The emotion is identified when people communicate their feelings, perceptions and expectations in verbal or non-verbal form. According to scholars (see, Gross & John, 2003; Richard & Gross, 2006) a state of emotion indicates the ability of a person to sense, monitor, justify, react or modulate their responses, but at a different capacity from a person to another. For example, in confronting stress, some people will cry or project sadness though unpleasant facial expressions or other behavior such as isolation. In addition, to establish beneficial relationships, appropriate communication skills are vital, such as communicating with a calm and logical message, using appropriate timing and channels, considering the other person's moods, perceptions and feelings, being aware and sensitive to different cultural clues and always being ready for any negative responses such as rejection, comments and so forth.

5. **Expression rules**. There are situations in which people should or should not express their emotion. For example, being humble rather than rebellious is a choice when a subordinate is being accused of a mistake by a superior. People need to understand, be aware and sensitive to the situations, timing and needs to display appropriate emotions. In the high-context culture of Asia, social status, ranking and hierarchy determine the intensity and acceptable protocol for showing emotions and gaining respect, trust, obedience and loyalty.

6. **Persuasion**. As mentioned earlier, emotions are a medium to convey and display messages about feelings, perceptions and expectations. Emotions could emphasize the message, to persuade or convince the other about particular needs and wants. Emotions are transferable and shared among people. For example, a person who tells a joke to show joy will be able to share the feeling with others when people start laughing.

In summary, there are elements that shape individual states of emotion, including societal and cultural customs and openness to affective reactions (joy, fear, surprise, anger, disgust and sadness). In addition, adequate interpersonal knowledge and skills are vital to express appropriate emotions (reappraisal or suppression) to ensure harmonious interpersonal relations and communication.

SKILLS OF EMOTIONAL EXPRESSION

Expressing emotion appropriately is important to avoid, reduce or eliminate interpersonal conflict, crisis, difficulty and violence. Negative consequences engendered by inappropriate cognitive (thinking), affective (emotions) and behavioural responses make interpersonal communication and relationship is a difficult process to handle. These difficulties create uncertainty, ambiguity, stress, anxiety, frustration, and depression. People's specific situational and emotional complexities depend on his/her personal cognitive and affective strength. Thus, sufficient skills to regulate the emotions are necessary to establish beneficial interpersonal relations and communication.

Matsumoto (2006) defined emotion regulation as an ability to manage and modify one's emotional reactions to achieve goal-oriented outcomes. Emotional regulation is one of the psychological skills (other than coping, mood regulation and psychological defense) that gave identical psycho-physiological impact to the individual differences (Gross, 1998; Ross, Richard & John, 2006). According to Gross and John (2003), effectiveness of the interpersonal communication and relationship is determined by the ability of a person to reappraise or suppress an emotion. Emotional reappraisal and suppression will be discussed in the following section.

Reappraisal Vs Suppression

Specifically, a common use of emotion regulation strategy that shows the individual differences can be classified as reappraisal (antecedent-focus) and suppression (response-focus) (Gross, 1998). The reappraisal strategy takes place before a person displays the emotion reaction. According to Gross (2001) the cognitive *reappraisal* form of emotional regulation comprises a situation selection, situation modification, deployment and cognitive change. On the other hand, *suppression* entails a modulation of emotional responses. Experiential, behavioural and physiological stipulation in laboratory research has demonstrated that reappraisal and suppression are effective mechanisms in regulating the expression of behavioural emotion but may have different adaptive consequences (Gross, 1998). In particular, reappraisers will reduce the experiential and behavioural components of negative emotional impact by reassessing the behaviour and reaction received. On the other hand, suppressors will reduce the behavioural expression of negative emotional impact by portraying a different expression, predominately by showing a positive state of actions and responses (Gross, 1998, 2001; Gross & John, 2003; Gross & Levenson, 1993).

EMOTIONAL INTELLIGENCE (EI)

There are studies (see, Goldman, 2001) that conceptualize the ability to regulate emotion as Emotional Intelligence (EI) and Emotional Quotient (EQ). Both terms refer to the individual emotional competency ability to understand and regulate their state of emotions. In particular, EI refers to the capability to understand, perceive, evaluate and control the affective responses of emotion. The states of emotions are perceived as part of individual personality shaped by socio-cultural background. However, in certain circumstances there are forms of emotion that can be learned, changed, developed, and treated. For example, anger or high-temper can be reduced and treated with appropriate motivation and psychological training. According to Mayer and Salovey (1990), EI is a part of social intelligence that specifies the ability to monitor self and the other's feelings and emotional reactions. EI uses the responses received as a guide to think rationally, taking appropriate actions for well-being. There are four sequential elements of EI that range from basic to higher states of emotion and involve psychologically integrated processes (Salovey & Mayer, 1997).

1. **Perceiving emotions**. A person needs to be aware of, and accurately learn, the emotional clues portrayed by the others. Ability to interpret the message received and give appropriate emotional response is important to avoid misunderstanding and interpersonal conflict. Emotional cues and reactions involve understanding of verbal and nonverbal signals. Furthermore, facial expression, body gesture and movement give some significant signals of the needs of emotional reactions.

2. **Reasoning with emotions**. Once notified by the communication clues from the others, reasoning ability (to accurately interpret the message) activates the thinking and cognitive systems. Experience,

knowledge, skills, specific frame of references and socio-cultural background (values, norms and beliefs) help a person to interpret the message and react with appropriate emotions. Furthermore, feelings and emotions assist an individual to justify the need to react and gives accurate feedback or responses.

3. **Understanding emotions.** Emotional responses are perceived as a support system to emphasize the written or verbal message with a varying magnitude of tone, voice, speed, length and clarity. Different forms of emotion may carry a variety of meanings. For example, a rough and loud voice when angry or soft voice to show love and joy. Some people show emotions that require further analysis of the cause of the reactions. For example, people who keep quiet or are silent (unusual behaviour) might mean that he/she is disgusted, angry, sad, in need of privacy or have experienced something personal in his/her life.

4. **Managing emotions.** Ability to regulate appropriate emotion is a key of the EI. Portraying and responding to the others' emotion accurately is crucial in order to establish mutual interpersonal relations and communication. DeVito (2009) proposed a SCREAM analogy as a method to manage anger and emotion.

   a. **S:** Refers to *self.* A person needs to realize, be aware and sensitive to the importance of responding to the others' emotion. For example, we can ask 'is it worth shouting as a sign of anger?'

   b. **C:** Refers to the suitable *context* of showing an emotion. The context includes place, time, event, situation or status of the others.

   c. **R:** Refers to the *receiver.* Whether a person is the right person to express emotions to. For example, it is inappropriate to show anger (using a harsh and loud voice) to the boss, cursing a mistake that we did not make.

   d. **E:** Refers to the *effect* and consequences of the emotion being expressed.

   e. **A:** Refers to the *aftermath* and long-term effect of the emotion being expressed.

f. **M**: Refers to the *message*. The accuracy, completeness, suitability and interpretability of the emotion expressed determine the effectiveness of the communication. For example, some people cry, which can be interpreted as a signal of sadness but may show joy.

EMOTIONAL QUOTIENT (EQ)

We need to make decisions all our lifetime. The decision could be simple or complex, easy or difficult, important or insignificant. The ability to estimate and predict the result could be influenced by a person's emotional state. Appropriate decisions and emotion regulation will determine the effectiveness of interpersonal relations and communication, and goal attainment. Hence, making effective decisions depends on the ability to understand a personal EQ. In particular, EQ is a method to measure an individual level of emotional intelligence. Comparatively, EI refers to the ability of a person to regulate the emotion (responding to the other's emotion). Likewise, EQ indicates an ability to sense, understand, manage and apply emotions to produce effective decisions, persuasion and productivity. Positive EQ indicates the ability of a person to: manage stress, communicate effectively, empathize with others, overcome problems and conflict, and obtain the beneficial relationships with others. EQ focuses on the impact of motions towards the understanding about intrapersonal (ability to understand oneself) and interpersonal (ability to understand others) relationship. There are five areas or attributes of EQ:

1. **Self-awareness**. In order to keep beneficial relationships with others, it is important for a person to recognize and understand his/her own moods, emotions, drives, needs and personality. An emotion could affect a person's thoughts, behaviour, and productivity.

2. **Self-management** (regulation). Maturity, experience, knowledge and skills will form a person's ability to control the emotions, feelings and moods which influence their expression and behaviour. It is vital for a person to analyze and justify a decision before portraying emotions or taking action. Hence, a clear message and positive drives (motivational forces) enable a person to pursue goals and establish beneficial relations with others.

3. **Motivation**. Life is just like a balloon: after some time it will shrink. Hence, we need to re-pump air into the balloon to keep it bigger. Thus, motivation is a force to develop and sustain momentum and achieve goals and success. Motivated people usually have a higher magnitude of EQ and are productive and efficient. Positive advice, success stories and rewards are examples to develop and sustain motivation.

4. **Social awareness and skills**. Understanding the socio-cultural background of the society will help to manage relationships and build positive social networks, especially in strange places.

5. **Relationship management** (empathy). Empathy helps people to feel socially comfortable and avoid interpersonal conflict, uncertainty and difficulties. Moreover, empathy indicates an ability to understand the emotional signs of others and thus manage the relationship. The capability to portray appropriate emotions helps to develop and maintain good relationships, inspire and influence others, and manage conflict.

Additionally, to have a good life with others, EQ is a pre-requisite to deal with life and social complexity especially anxiety, uncertainty and stress. Furthermore, sufficient EQ bolsters performance, productivity, physical and mental health, effective communication and beneficial relationships. Keys to gaining an acceptable EQ include work-life balance, rationality, a minimal stress level and a positive state of mind. In particular, there are five key skills to develop higher magnitude of EQ these are:

1. EQ skill 1: **Stress reduction**. Relaxation, calm, creativity, being innovative, staying focused and meditating are keys to control and manage stress and other life pressure (such as fatigue).

2. EQ skill 2: **Emotional awareness**. EQ indicates an ability of a person to recognize and manage affective expression of emotions. Awareness of emotional changes (such as anger, joy, sadness, fear, disgust and surprise) influences positive thoughts and action.

3. EQ skill 3: **Silent cues**. Effective interpersonal communication and relationship require some significant ability to connect with others using appropriate nonverbal communication skills. In general, interpersonal conflict occurs with the inability of a person to interpret accurately gestures and other nonverbal cues. The nonverbal signals indicate pull factors (interest, trust, respect, excitement, enthusiasm or desire for connection) or push factors (fear, confusion, distrust, annoyance, denial or rejection). Hence, staying focused, paying attention, making appropriate eye and body contact, and being aware of nonverbal signals (such as facial expression, posture and gestures, distance, tone of voice, interpersonal contact (touching, rubbing, tapping), timing and pace of conversation are important skills to eliminate interpersonal difficulties.

4. EQ skill 4: **Sense of humour**. Joy and happiness elevate emotion and moods, and are perceived as an antidote to the stress. Jokes, play and laughter seem to be easy tools to create joy and happiness in relationships with others.

5. EQ skill 5: **Positive solutions**. Ability to solve problems and conflict with a positive attitude and confidence determine a person's level of EQ. Problem solving with healthy, constructive, positive, creative and innovative solutions will foster freedom and mutual relationships with others.

EQ is used by organizations to assess employee performance, their ability to works under pressure, resolve conflict, self-confidence, personality, attitude and aptitude. Furthermore, EQ can be used as a tool to understand and assess people's behaviours, managerial styles, human resources management, and planning and development skills (such as job profiling, recruitment, interviewing and selection, training and evaluation).

To summarize, emotions (EI or EQ) are important to balance life satisfaction, success and goal attainment. Specifically, emotions regulate a person's feeling and actions in order to establish mutual interpersonal relations and communication.

7 Power in Communication and Relationship

Power is an ability to influence what other people think, hear or do. This process of persuasion needs a certain magnitude of power. The power may derive from status, rank, hierarchy or physical force. In addition, soft power (kindness, integrity, appearance and honesty) can be used to convince people about their needs and wants, and gain trust, obedience and respect. The goals are achieved through empowerment of authority that shows the power to implement the decision, order or instruction. In interpersonal relations and communication, power plays a role that blends the relationships. A successful interdependent relationship is established when a person exerts greater power (by skills, education or finance) over the other.

PRINCIPLES OF POWER

Power is a psychological force that may affect positive or negative outcomes. Power is acquired through cognitive learning processes, personal experiences or it may have been assigned. Power could be a medium to portray an individual's personality, inherited since birth. For example, a baby will cry to show protest, begging to get food or attention. For adult, past negative experience makes some people autocratic in decision making. On the other hand, positive experiences could make people more diplomatic when persuading people to follow orders and instructions. Lastly, assigned power is obtained through position, status and hierarchy, especially within the organizational structure. There are six principles that explain the role of power in interpersonal relations and communication.

1. **Inequality.** People have different magnitudes of power, psychologically and physically. Some people are more powerful than others. For example, people who share a similar demographic background (such as gender, age, race, religion) do not have equal physical strength. Similarly, some people are rewarded and receive job promotion faster than others. Inequality of power can be used to obtain sympathy, help, support and protection from those who have power and authority. On the other hand, power is often perceived as connected to violence, misuse, exploitation and discrimination.

2. **Shared.** In order to have a harmonious relationship, power can be shared to reduce tension and simplify work. For example, the husband could do work that requires physical strength, such as moving furniture while the wife does floor sweeping and cleaning. Besides, delegating power could increase the other's self-esteem, and motivation, so work is accomplished faster. Sharing of power can reduce competition, increase productivity and produce better outcomes. Consolidation, amalgamation, consortium, alliance, partnership, merger and acquisition are among corporate strategies that combine several similar or different business units to form a single business power. For example, alliances between Continental Airlines and United Airlines to form the United-Continental, Time Warner and AOL, Daimler Benz and Chrysler, and Sime Darby (merging Guthrie and Golden Hope).

3. **Frequency.** The amount of power can be increased or decreased dependant on the situation, need and goal. For example, the wife could utilize her persuasive power to ask her husband to buy jewelry for her. Power may be applied to reinforce, persuade or convince the other to give respect, obedience and loyalty. Needs and goals compliance indicate the successful use of power.

Contrarily, resistance is received when power used has no effect on others. Particularly, misuse of power causes negative responses such as rejection, denial, crime, rebellion, quarrelling or fighting. Hence, power will decrease or disappear with unsuccessful control over others.

4. **Privilege.** There is a possibility that a person use the power to cover his/her insecurity or incompetency (psychologically or physically). He/she might use the power to overcome their anxiety, uncertainty or inferiority. For example, a robber or snatcher will use physical strength to commit the crime. However, knowledge, experience, skill and luck give an advantage to some people to gain power and authority. For example, a supervisor being promoted to a manager based on his/her work performance. Particularly, having power and controlling others is perceived as a privilege.

5. **Cultural.** The amount of power owned by a person could differ from one culture to another. In Western countries, human rights and equality between genders are the main principles governing individual and social power. However, in other cultures, elements of socio-cultural background (such as gender, age, race, ranking, status and hierarchy) differentiate levels of power and social position. For example, in most Arab countries, a man has dominant power in the marital relationship and is freely involved in economic, political and socio-cultural activities. However, Arab women have limited opportunity to socialize, work or voice their opinions without permission granted from their husbands or guardians. In a monarchial system, the eldest is prioritized to lead and make decisions although younger may be better suited to these tasks.

TYPES OF POWER

There are various types of power related to interpersonal relations and communication. The use of power varies according to need, position, time, location, event and goal. However, the main purpose of power is to influence others. Thus, persuasion and control is the key to determine the effectiveness of power. Sufficient persuasive skills give benefits to a person by allowing them to control the interpersonal relationship. There are six types of power in the interpersonal relationships:

1. **Referent**. The social status, hierarchy or rank of a person gives referent power. Being a referent, a person has the power to make people want to follow and admire him. A person who has referent power is a role-model or idol to certain others.

2. **Legitimate**. An authority empowered will bring legitimate power. With certain job positions, a person might use legitimate power to influence or control the others' behaviour, thinking and feelings. Legitimate power is created based on the belief system that a person might have automatic power once they achieve a certain social level or position. Examples are teachers, professors, religious leaders, police officers and managers.

3. **Expert**. A person has power when owning exclusive knowledge, skill, experience and expertise in a specific field. For example, a doctor is an expert in medical knowledge, a mechanic in vehicle repairs, an architect in structure design and so forth. We would not refer a problem or need clarification to these people without knowing their expert background.

4. **Informational** (persuasion). A person has a persuasive power when seen by the other as having a good command of knowledge and information shared. People will believe the stories, orders and instructions given when they have been effectively persuaded and convinced about something. For example, a product or service is purchased after being explained or demonstrated by the sales promoter.

5. **Reward**. Gifts, presents, perks, tokens of appreciation, appraisal and acknowledgement are examples of reward power. Giving a reward enables the authority to change the productivity and interpersonal relationship. For example, a ten month's bonus is promised if the targeted sales are achieved. This promise would encourage subordinates to work hard in order to get the rewards.

6. **Coercive**. In contrast to reward power, punishment is given when the goal is not achieved, or need is not fulfilled. Normally, a superior has coercive power over others to punish a mistake. For example, in Saudi it was two days salary cut for every day late back from a holiday. This rules enforced to ensure the worker's commit to their job.

These referent, legitimate, expert, informational, reward and coercive types of power may give positive or negative effects. Positive outcomes are obtained when both sides are happy and satisfied after has been used. On the other hand, negative outcomes (such as rejection, quarrel or fight) are created when a person misuses power. For example, reward power can be seen as bribes.

PERSONAL POWER

As humans, we use personal power in order to fulfill our needs. Personality and past experiences build a personal drive to excel in life. Besides, personal power helps an individual to build self-esteem and achieve a higher level of self-actualization needs (reference: Maslow's Hierarchy of Needs). Credibility, image, personality and self-efficacy are perceived as elements of personal competency that gives personal power. Trust, respect, obedience and loyalty are benefits gained through appropriate use of personal power. Credibility is perceived as the main drive to develop personal power. Credibility is perceived as the personal quality of being believed and trusted. There are three elements of credibility:

1. **Competence**. Knowledge, skills and experiences differentiate the credibility of one person from another. Expertise in a particular area can be used to gain trust, respect, believability, influence and control over others.

2. **Character** (personality). Character is personal attributes also referred to as personality. Personality differentiates patterns of thinking (cognitive), feelings (affective) and behaviour of one person from another. Individual personality is built and influenced by socio-cultural elements (norms, values, beliefs and attitudes). According to the Social Learning Theory (see Bandura,

1977), a human's character is developed through the imitation process from his/her surroundings since birth. Hence, knowing the place of origin and socio-cultural background is essential to understand people's character.

3. **Charisma.** Charisma is a psychological element that portrays individual distinctive and favourable values. People will judge a person's value through his/her morals, attitude and aptitude. Attitude is an expression of individual goodwill, moods and motivational drives. Additionally, aptitude is a component of competency that indicates the ability of a person to achieve a higher level of self-actualization needs (utilization of talent and mental wellness).

COMMUNICATION POWER

Power also exists in transmitting messages. Appropriate power embedded in the communication will establish effective interpersonal relations. Communication power refers to the art of composing messages that bring definite 'meaning' to confirm or change the receiver's thought, feeling, perception and behaviour. Communication power is paramount in a process of negotiation (compromising to achieve a satisfactory outcome), justification (needing clarification) and identity manipulation (persuasion). Power in communication can be found in various areas including speaking, writing, listening and nonverbal signals.

1. **Speaking.** Voice, tone and pace of spoken words have a different impact on the listener. For example, a soft voice with low volume indicates agreement to the conversed subject. On the other hand, a harsh voice with high pitch or tone could indicate anger or disagreement. However, interpretation of the spoken message is also dependent on the personality of a speaker and listener. In normal conditions, some people speak with a variety of tone and voices. Thus, it is important for the listener to understand the situation and personality of a person before engaging in extensive conversation. Power in communication is normally emphasized in the process of negotiation, manipulation, bargaining, convincing, criticizing or threatening.

2. **Writing**. The use of words, phrases and sentence structure, and format in written documents could result in a variety of interpretation. Completeness, clarity and accuracy of writing indicate the power, urgency and goal to achieve. Besides, different forms of writing give different messages and intentions, such as invitations, greetings, clarifications, petitions or threats (such as a writ of summons).

3. **Listening**. Effective communication cannot be achieved without active listening. Accurately interpreting the message includes not only the preached or spoken words but also nonverbal signals. Active listening is obtained when the listener gives appropriate attention and focus to the conversation. However, the amount of the interruption (such as temperature, venue and choice of communication medium) also plays a role to ensure effective communication.

4. **Nonverbal signals**. Appearance (outfits), body posture, gestures, distance from audience, movement and facial expression demonstrate an indirect message in interpersonal communication. These nonverbal signals are able to convey a message to show the power. For example, arm folding while talking may indicate a sign of resistance.

Particularly, power in communication is established through particular interpersonal communication and relationship skills (especially speaking, listening and writing) that will be discussed in the following chapter. In summary, power in interpersonal communication and relationship can give a positive or negative impression. The power could help to change the status quo, to improve or sustain the relationship. However, the lack of communication power may present a negative impression, and hinder interpersonal relations and communication. Therefore, acquiring sufficient communication knowledge, skills and experience is vital to determine the effectiveness of interpersonal relationships.

8 Communication and Relationship Skills

Skill is the capability to do something with a learned capacity, to produce high productivity. Skill can differentiate one person from another. A soft skill is a psychological ability, such as flirting with a girl, speed reading, or cursive writing. On the other hand, a craft skill requires physical ability to perform jobs such goldsmith, chef, ice decorator, or painter. Knowledge, passion, practice, experience, innovation, creativity and initiative are required to ensure quality outcomes of the skill. This chapter will discuss the general human ability to establish effective interpersonal relations and communication, including speaking, writing and listening.

SPEAKING SKILLS

Speaking is an action conveying a message (information, thought or feeling) through spoken language. The messages are composed with particular words, phrases and sentences that create a language. Socio-cultural and geographical areas generate different forms of language expression known as dialect, accent and slang. In particular, dialect is a form of language that belongs to a specific region or social group. Different rhyming language indicates slang or accent which differs regionally. Peculiar terminology or improper use of standard language will form a jargon. Examples of jargon are: pragmatics, posited, analogy, ontological, psychometric and so forth. Additionally, voice and tone play a role that affect the effectiveness of interpersonal relations and communication. Several speaking skills necessary to establish effective interpersonal communication and relationship include:

1. Pronouncing words and phrases clearly, especially with languages that have different tonal distinctions (such as Mandarin and Cantonese) and gender differences (words used to refer to men or women) like in Arabic.

2. Stressing appropriate rhythmic patterns (especially for slang or accent) to avoid misinterpretation. Pace of intonation might give various interpretations of the 'meaning'. Misuse of intonation could be perceived as arrogant, annoying or insulting.

3. Standard language has its own grammatical patterns, order and rules. Hence, learning the grammar (that forms appropriate phrases or sentences) is as important as the vocabulary of the language.

4. A language that has several dialects might have several different accents. For an instance:

    a. The same word with the same meaning but different intonation of pronunciation (flat, increasing or decreasing tone) such as 'highland' in British and American.
    b. The same word with the same meaning but different pronunciation. For example, the word 'seven' pronounced as 'say-ven' by someone from Great Britain but 'sea-ven' by a New Zealander.
    c. A different word but the same meaning, such as theatre vs cinema, flat vs apartment.

    To avoid miscommunication across culture, a person needs to be aware of and use the vocabulary of the particular language and dialect appropriately. However, copying the accent could be perceived as annoying or even an insult.

5. It is a speaker's obligation to make the conversation topic clear to the listener. Unclear or too much talking makes the communication fail, and the listener lose focus and interest. Hence, clarification and justification of ideas and information is needed, ideally supported by physical materials to highlight the main talking points.

6. For the speaker, observing the salient clues (gestures, expression, movement and distance from the audience) that may be used to emphasize or clarify to the talking point. As a listener, salient cues somehow could indicate the listeners' agreed, accept, confuse, lost, blur, reject, annoying, bored or disagreed.

In interpersonal communication, it is vital for a person to be sensitive to the situation and the background of the others in a conversation. Although the ability to speak a language (verbal or nonverbal) can be obtained through proper classroom language training, ground experience (ethnographic) or observation can help to develop the skill.

LISTENING SKILLS

Listening is a process of receiving verbal information. The purpose of listening is to be able to understand a message and respond appropriately. Understanding the message that we hear is dependent on many factors, such as semantics, types and level of noises. The complexity of the message also contributes to the effectiveness of the interpersonal communication. Interpersonal breakdown occurs due to the listener's unawareness, lack of focus or interest in the message. There are two forms of listening situations: interactive and non-interactive conversation. Interactive situations involve a face-to-face communication (dyad, interviews, meetings), or telephone video or voice calls or through internet (messaging using Skype or camera-to-camera messenger). Interactive sessions allow speaker and listener to communicate and clarify, repeat or request changes. In contrast, non-interactive sessions require only a listening process, such as listening to the radio, television, film, lecture, demonstration, presentation, public speaking and talk. Most of the non-interactive (and part of interactive communication session) do not require the listener to take immediate action or give prompt responses to the received message. Some people listen not because of the contents of the message but as a way of showing respect, or to avoid interpersonal relationship problems. Hence, several listening skills could help to establish effective interpersonal relations and communication:

1. To recognize the goal and purpose of the conversation or events.
2. To classify and differentiate the need of the message, such as informative or persuasive.
3. To identify the talking points (topics and ideas).
4. To recognize the language used (vocabulary, syntax, structure, grammar and patterns).
5. To recognize the language, dialect and accent.
6. To identify the seriousness of the sound, rhythm or tonal expression of mood (joy, fear, surprise, anger, disgust and sadness).
7. To observe and be sensitive to the salient socio-cultural clues (gestures, expression, movement and distance from audience), emotional and psychological signals (such as intentions, feeling and expectation).
8. To reasonably presume and predict the meaning from the context of the ideas.
9. To appropriately interpret the message.
10. To maintain interpersonal contact (such as eye contact and other non-verbal signs).
11. To appropriately adjust and adapt to communication changes, such as situations, context, events, intonation and voice.
12. To focus on the content of the message.
13. To control the level of noise within the environment.
14. Generally speaking, 'practise makes perfect' is the key to developing effective communication skills (listening, thinking, and wondering at the same time).

Listening is one of the mediums to establish a beneficial interpersonal relationship and communication. Active listening is a key to developing a mutual relationship. General rules to institute active listening will be discussed in the following section.

Active listening

Active listening completes the effective circle of communication and builds the relationship. The goal of active listening is to hear what other people are really saying. Active listening is useful to improve productivity, and to influence, persuade, convince or negotiate. A self and socio-cultural awareness are essential to establish good communication skills. Active listening is not simply obtained by paying attention to the speaker but involves full understanding of the entire message and communication process. Several active listening strategies to improve the effectiveness of interpersonal communication and relationship include:

1. *Timing.* Choosing the right time and right place to communicate is important in order to establish effective communication. For example, a serious communication is not supposed to be held when we are in a hurry, physically and mentally exhausted, angry or sick.

2. *Readiness.* Both speaker and listener have to be ready for communication. Concentration and an effective communication process are achieved once we are physically and mentally prepared. In addition, it is necessary for us to prepare in advance any clues about the message that we are going to receive or hear. Clues and preparation (research and notification) will help to minimize possible negative consequences such as shock or surprise about the information.

3. *Position.* The best physical position to establish effective listening is dyad and face-to-face (sitting or standing, looking directly at the speaker's face). For non-interactive conversation, a person needs to be relaxed, sitting or standing properly and not doing another job at the same time.

4. *Concentration.* It is important that the listener pays appropriate attention, focuses on the talking point and acknowledges the message. The main goal of active listening is to listen. A key to establish effective listening is through giving and maintaining an appropriate eye contact, making both speaker and listener comfortable. Thus, they need mutual concentration and

determination to play a role as a good listener, giving verbal or non-verbal responses when invited to do so by the speaker. Therefore, communication awareness and sensitivity is vital to encourage effective communication and develop better interpersonal relationships.

5. **Control noises.** Intervention of unexpected or uncontrollable noises detracts from the communication process. Hence, a listener needs to reduce or eliminate the noises (for example in a construction area) or request for alternative clarification (when speaker has a semantic problem or difficulty with communication devices). Some alternative to the communication problem includes use of translators, a third party or written devices. Interruption could frustrate the speaker. Thus, allow the speaker to convey his entire message before providing any feedback. Other than external noises, open-mindedness also helps to eliminate difficulties in relationship without making judgements or assumptions about the speaker. Furthermore, the listener needs to minimize unhelpful internal distractions such as health issues, moods and expectations.

6. **Salient cues.** Include facial expression, body gestures, posture, distance from the speaker and movement. As explained before, salient cues might give a positive or negative message such as seduction, attraction, rejection, annoyance or disgust. Similarly, listeners also need to maintain good manners and control his/her own salient cues.

7. **Encouragement.** The listener can help to create a comfortable conversation by giving agreement signs to the speaker. Examples of encouragement signs include: keeping an open and inviting posture, appropriate use of facial expression, nodding occasionally and giving supportive comments such as "yes", and "aha". Even though the listener might disagree with the speaker, he should let the speaker finish talking before giving his opinion.

8. **Feedback.** As discussed in Chapter Two, feedback is required to ensure an effective and complete communication circle. Feedback

is important to filter, confirm, clarify and judge the message. Besides, appropriate feedback could establish understanding, rapport, respect, and trust, which enhance the mutual relationship. The feedback could come in a form of agreement, repeating and paraphrasing the talking points, comments, suggestions or summarizing. The listener should assert his opinions and responses respectfully, not by attacking the speaker with comments that will be perceived as humiliating. In certain circumstances, showing emotions (smiling, laughing, crying or being silent) and body language is perceived sufficient to provide feedback.

By being an active listener, we possibly will create worthy relationships, be appreciated and be respected. Fostering the skill of active listening brings greater intimacy and chemistry in interpersonal relations and communication. Besides, listening is a soft skill that builds self-confidence and self esteem. Additionally, it reduces the possibility of social and emotional disturbance and the curse of showing ignorance, denial, disgust or annoyance. Plant the active listening skill by listening to others as we would want to be listened to by others.

WRITING SKILLS

Writing is an ability and process of conveying written messages. Writing is simply done by scribbling words, using a basic knowledge of an alphabet and how to form phrases. However, producing informative and persuasive writing requires particular knowledge and skills. Writing skills seem to be complicated and hard, especially for non-native speakers of a language. The presentation of ideas in properly structured grammar is a major challenge. There are several writing strategies to establish writing credibility and convince the reader about the message. They include:

1. Assessing the reader's background to identify their interest. Knowing the reader's background will help organize the ideas. Besides, an appropriate writing style is important to address the reader correctly.

2. Choosing an appropriate channel and medium of writing communication, such as email, on paper (formal/informal letters, memoranada, flyers, brochures or catalogues), bunting, or advertisement board.

3. Choosing and using the correct form of words.
4. Using correct vocabulary or choice of words.
5. Writing in a complete sentence and meaningful phrases.
6. Ensuring correct spelling and punctuation.
7. Observing standard format of the document (such as formal/ informal letter, legal document, reports, books or journals).
8. Observing a suitable technical format of the text writing (such as the main title, headings, subheadings, bullet points, numbering, margin, spacing and so forth).
9. Using appropriate sentence and paragraph structure (for example introduction, main ideas, supporting ideas and justification, conclusion).
10. Checking for correct grammar (such as tenses, voice, gender, participles and prepositions).
11. Ensuring a logical flow of ideas.
12. Providing sufficient references, acknowledgement and bibliographical citations in order to avoid plagiarism.
13. Having the writing proofread by a native speaker of the language. Proofreaders are able to help spot any flaws and mistakes in writing, such as contents, formats and grammar.

In addition to the writing strategies as above, there are several elements of writing that could encourage effective interpersonal communication. The written messages could give various impressions and be interpreted in many ways, depending on the reader's frame of reference and other cognitive and emotional factors. Therefore, several aspects to observe in writing include:

1. Compose messages while taking into consideration other people's way of thinking is vital to avoid misinterpretation. Respecting the other's sensitivity is important to avoid racism, ethnocentrism or arrogance (especially regarding issues related to human rights, dignity, religious belief and sovereignty).
2. Plan and organise the ideas (for example the use of a check-list, mind-mapping, table of content or outline) to guide the writing process.
3. Persuasive writing needs some element of empathy to catch the reader's attention, interest and support.

4. Focus only on a single theme. For example, this book is written to discuss the elements that relate to interpersonal relations and communication.

5. Use an appropriate tone in the message to avoid misinterpretation. Writing tone (through the use of words and phrases) can display emotion (such as anger, joy, sadness, fear, disgust and surprise), urgency, reflections or notifications.

6. Visual aids (such as pictures, page design, colour and other multimedia icons) are able to make the document visually attractive. A fancy document is able to keep the reader engaged and curious especially in advertising and informative flyers, brochures or pamphlets. However, over-use of design may overshadow the main message. Thus, short, simple and precise notes are better able to produce quick responses from readers when an urgent and prompt reply is needed. In technical writing, the use of graphs and charts helps to replace wordy passages and break up the text.

Special writing skills

There are some writing abilities that give extra value to the writing. Impressive technical and comprehensive writing could catch the reader's interest. Properly conveying a written message by adhering to the standard writing format creates credibility and gains respect for the writer. Besides, the way messages are composed may portray the personality of the writer. There are several special writing skills include:

1. ***Cursive writing.*** This is a style of hand-writing where the words are conjoined in a flowing manner. Cursive writing is also known as script, joined-up writing, joint writing, linking, running writing or handwriting. The main purpose of cursive writing is to make writing faster. In general, cursive writing refers to techniques in combining or joining the letters. In languages such as Arabic and Latin, many letters in a word are connected; this makes a single word a complex stroke.

2. ***Short-hand.*** Stenography is the act or writing process in shorthand. In shorthand writing, the Romanic letters are written in abbreviated symbols that simplify the words and phrases. In particular, shorthand is a method to increase writing speed and

save time when collecting and recording information. Shorthand notes are typically used to record lengthy but important information obtained from oral speaking. The information is later transcripted into proper Romanic writing (normal or longhand writing). Shorthand skills were part of secretarial and journalism training requirements. However, the invention and advancement of recording gadgets (such as video and voice recorder) and computer software with encoded technology (from voice to words) has replaced the shorthand function. Although shorthand is rarely used today, it can be useful as a secret code in dairy writing.

3. *Creative writing.* Writers' thoughts, feelings, perceptions and emotions are expressed in this most pleasant form of reading material. Creative writing can attract the reader's attention and leave an emotional and psychological impact in their mind. The ideas are conveyed in a manner that differs from the normal straightforward writing of professional, journal, academic and technical documents or reports. The stories are crafted based on the writer's personal experiences, socio-cultural observations or imagination. The themes and genres of creative writing include folklore, fiction (such as poetry, humour, novels, short stories) or non-fiction (such as biographies), script writing and so forth. Specifically, creative writing is focused on narrative and character development.

4. *Professional (technical) writing.* There are documents prepared for special purposes by experts in the special area. Professional writers are related to a variety of specialist occupations such as journalist, web content manager, marketer, advertiser, accountant, architect, medical doctor, attorney and business executive. Examples of professional documents include an architect's blueprint, a lawyer's legal instruments (writ of summons, agreements and client correspondence), an accountant's audited financial report, a market and economic analysis, a contract, memoranda, and business letters. Some professional documents use special formats, terms and vocabulary to represent particular conditions. For example, 'crocodile crack', 'ad valorem', 'affidavit', 'bona fide' and many others.

5. *Academic writing.* Articles or essays are pieces of writing expressing the author's personal views on academic matters. The purpose of academic writing is to educate and provide new insight, improve the state of knowledge through original research, form a political manifesto and so on. Academic writing includes: learned arguments; recollections and re-search; behavioural observations; and reasoned conclusions. An academic essay includes expository, descriptive, narrative and argumentative (persuasive) writing. *Expository* writing requires writers to investigate and evaluate ideas and express their argument precisely but concisely. Expository writing involves comparing, contrasting, defining and investigating cause-effect relationships. *Descriptive* writing involves an explanation and description of an object, person, place, experience, emotion or other processes. For example, a describing the formation of birds on their seasonal migrations.

In contrast with the descriptive form, *narrative* writing expresses the sequential plots of a story. Normally, the nature of narrative writing is anecdotal experiential, and personal. For example, the process of obtaining national independence for a country; a family vacation to Queenstown, Lake Wanaka and Fiordland in New Zealand; or the best-remembered birthday party. Lastly, *argumentative* (persuasive) writing requires writers to investigate ideas, issues or problems. Written arguments involve a process of collecting, ordering and evaluating evidence. The writer is challenged to produce a concise but clear, complete, logical opinion and argument. In order to gain trust, and convince people about the posited ideas, empirical research (interviews, surveys, observations, or experiments) is required to collect supporting evidence.

Apart from the four academic styles discussed as above, there is another form of academic writing that contains distinctive formats. It includes term papers, theses or dissertations, research papers (conceptual and empirical) and coursework. Different institutions might outline different formats of reporting. However, the Modern Language Association (MLA) and the American Psychological Association (APA) are the most commonly used styles and formats to use when writing papers, especially within the liberal arts, humanities and social sciences areas.

READING SKILLS

Reading is the receptive skill in interpersonal relations and communication. People not only read the written materials, but also comprehend the invisible meaning behind the written words. Reading is interdependent with writing, reading and speaking. For example, we have to read before we can write, we read while writing, and re-read after writing is completed. Reading can become a complicated and difficult process, especially when dealing with a foreign language. In addition, reading printed materials is insufficient without comprehending the socio-cultural background of the particular language. For example, international business successes in the Chinese market are influenced by the level of understanding of the concept of *'mianxi'* (face saving).

The purpose of a reading activity is to extract the key information, verify existing knowledge or identify knowledge gaps for further improvement. However, knowledge and experience is very important to institute spectacular reading skills. Other than job reasons, people read for enjoyment, as a spare time activity, or to update themselves with recent states of affairs (national or international socio-economic and political scenarios). The purpose of reading and types of text also determine the appropriate techniques and approach to reading comprehension. For example, ontological analysis, understanding the facts and cause-effect relationship of the idea is needed when reviewing the literature on scientific academic research. Recognising words and overall meaning of poetic structure are preferred when reading poetry for enjoyment, without a need to know the precise detail of the ideas.

Reading activities involve some integrated and interactive processes between the reader and the text. Understanding the words, phrases, sentences and paragraphs are important to identify the meaning of the message appropriately. Sufficient knowledge, skills, techniques and strategies (such as a linguistic, sociolinguistic and strategic competence) are required to comprehend the meaning. The typical reading method passages the text word by word, stopping at the end of each sentence to guess the meaning (especially with unfamiliar or unknown vocabulary). However, this technique not only slows the reading process but makes the reader lose interest and discourages him from completing the reading.

Hence, other strategies are useful to increase effective reading. These include:

1. Reviewing titles, section headings and captions to identify the main idea, and sense the contents and structures using skimming and scanning methods.
2. Recognising vocabulary (the meaning and use in context), writing styles and formats.
3. Associating the meaning of words with written symbols.
4. Distinguishing between the main ideas and supporting details.
5. Detecting and recognising grammatical structure, sentence constituents and syntactic patterns.
6. Predicting the meaning of the unfamiliar, unknown or complicated vocabulary through prior knowledge and context of the subjects and ideas in the text.
7. Paraphrasing to check comprehension, by restating the information and ideas in the text.

Moreover, reading is essential for knowledge enhancement. People read to obtain information and it supports the learning process. Other than learning specific knowledge, reading can be used as a medium to learn a language (vocabulary, grammar, sentences and discourse structure). Several skills to improve reading capability and effectiveness include:

1. **Styles of reading**. People have different interests and preferences of reading materials. There are three general styles of reading that can be used to read on different occasions and for different purposes.

    a. *Scanning*. This technique is used for a specific focus. Readers will glance at the text, only looking at specific sections in the passage. The reader is normally searching for key words or highlighted headings. For example, 'appointments', 'TV guide' and 'sport' are specific sections in the newspaper where that subject can be read in detail. Besides, headings and subheading assist the reader to spot relevant words or phrases. For example, in an academic journal, a researcher may only be interested in the findings section and can ignore the rest of the article. However, without specific clues to locate the information, there are sections in the reading materials that provide overviews of the whole text. For example, the abstract, preface, introduction, first or last paragraph of the particular chapter or article, and conclusion of a book or article.

b. *Skimming.* This is a reading technique to identify the general idea before reading or studying the article intensively. Readers will quickly spot the main idea (by running their eyes over the text) and skip over the detail and other supporting ideas. It is not essential in skimming to understand in detail the meaning of the words, phrases or whole text. Skimming is useful to preview a passage before reading in detail or analysing the information. Skimming also helps to refresh the memory or understand a passage after detailed reading. Skimming is used to identify specific knowledge or information needed, or as an assessment tool to judge the relevance and use of the reading material. For example, before making a decision to buy a book, we judge the contents of the book by scanning certain chapters or sections to decide whether the book is worth buying. Other examples of the skimming process include: quickly skimming a newspaper to find the general news of the day; glancing at a magazine to discover articles to read in detail; and quickly getting information from travel brochures.

2. **Active reading.** Is an intensive reading by being involved in the reading material entirely. Active reading requires a high level of concentration on the subject matters of the material. Rather than reading the material blindly, there are various techniques to help active reading.

a. *Underlining and highlighting* the main points. The reader needs to use his/her knowledge and experience to decide the important ideas and information written in the reading materials. Visual learners may use different colours to highlight or underline different ideas and aspects in the article. The physical action of highlighting keeps the reader engaged and active.

b. Jotting down or noting the **key words** in certain paragraphs or headings in the passage. Every paragraph should explain different ideas or provide different information. Hence, several key words can be used to summarise the article.

c. In serious reading, the reader could ask or note several **questions** that they expect the reading material to answer. For example, if we are interested in specific methodology, the questions might ask how the author of the article collected the data, his/her sampling frame, measurements, data analysis procedures, and so forth. Listing the questions helps to guide the reader on the purpose of reading and determine the relevancy of the materials.

d. To examine their understanding of the reading material, the reader should be able to **summarize** the article in his/her own words. Paraphrasing, reporting and synthesising are techniques to simplify the information. Furthermore, summarizing is an effective technique to shorten a lengthy article and is useful for future reference. The text should be re-skimmed to check the accuracy of the summary and add any important missing information.

3. **Speed reading**. The pace and speed of the reading influences the effectiveness of the reading process. However, speed reading improves reading interest, especially for lengthy, academic and technical material. The materials, mind, eyes, fingers (for beginners), and reading position all play a role in increasing reading speed. The **SQ3R** method to increase reading speed was introduced by Robinson in his book "Effective Study" (1946). It makes five suggestions as follows:

a. **Survey**. The reader needs to gather as much information as possible. Sufficient material can help the reader to focus on the words when the reading process is started. The title of the material (books, articles) gives clues about the reading subject. Extract the key points by reading the introduction or conclusion of the article. Some articles have an abstract that summarises the whole material. Look at headings and subheadings to see the structure and the information arrangement of the material. The Table of Contents is a short-cut for readers to identify the structure of the material, especially books. Observe the visual aids (graphs, charts, tables) and reading aids (footnotes, endnotes, italics, boldface, underlines) that may indicate the important points highlighted by the authors.

b. *Question*. As mentioned earlier, questions beforehand can help readers engage with the reading process. The reader's mind will focus on the article in order to find the answers to the questions. The boldface headings give a clue which sections will answer the questions.

c. *Read*. Reading the passage by keeping questions in mind will direct focus and concentration. Once a question is answered, there are possibilities that additional sub-questions may arise. For example, a main reading question may be: 'what is the researcher's sampling frame?' If the answer is 'by using respondents', sub-questions could subsequently include: 'how did the researcher recruit the respondents?', 'how did the researcher ensure respondents' participation?', or 'how did he ensure respondents' honesty when contributing responses?'.

d. *Recall*. Before moving to the next question or section in the passage, pause a while to consider the previous questions. Recalling the previous questions and reading information helps to increase reading comprehension.

e. *Review*. Once reading is completed, assemble all the notes and go through all the questions. Paraphrase or summarise the readings points to answer the questions. Review the passage and refresh the memory if the questions are not answered. Otherwise, the article may not provide the information needed. Furthermore, note-taking is another skill needed to enhance reading effectiveness.

4. **Reading navigation aids**. There are several reading navigation aids crafted by authors in their articles. Navigation aids help the

writer to organize their writing. Similarly, the reader can spot the arrangement of ideas by recognising a sequential signal. For example, the use of bullet points, numbering and other indications of ideas such as 'firstly, secondly, lastly', 'several elements', 'characteristics', and so forth. Moreover, there is salient information hidden in the passage that could influence the reader's and focus. For example, the ways authors elaborate the ideas could portray bias. Information could be influenced by the author's political ideology, religious belief and socio-cultural background.

5. **Words and vocabulary.** To increase reading comprehension, a person can choose to use a more comprehensive dictionary rather than a pocket dictionary. Besides, longer articles or more complex material could give wider perspectives and improve the reader's vocabulary.

Reading Comprehension

Moving on, the reader needs to ensure the quality time spent for reading results in comprehending, extracting and gaining knowledge from the material. Reading comprehension indicates the level of understanding grasped from the meaning of the text. Comprehending and understanding the printed message are stimulated through the techniques and strategies discussed earlier. Expected comprehension is achieved when the reader is able to paraphrase, re-explain or take further action as required. Specifically, comprehension skills used in reading indicate the ability of the reader to use prior knowledge and context to make sense of the reading activities. Indications of reading comprehension are when the reader is:

1. Able to remember most of the important points, sources and other related details from the reading material.
2. Able to express, interpret and evaluate the ideas, opinions and information.
3. Able to match, connect, contrast or synthesize the extracted information with other knowledge sources.
4. Able to adjust prior knowledge with the ideas extracted and construe the new information from a different perspective.

Continuing on, according to Harvey and Goudvis (2000), there are several types of strategies to increase comprehension. The strategies include the ability of the readers to make connections with prior and new knowledge, ask questions, visualize, determine text importance, make inferences (judging the information) and synthesize (compare and combine new information with existing knowledge). Among others, Harvey and Goudvis (2000) explain in detail the techniques to determine text importance as follows:

1. Distinguish between what is essential and what is interesting.
2. Distinguish between fact and opinion.
3. Determine cause-and-effect relationships.
4. Compare and contrast ideas or information.
5. Distinguish themes, opinions or perspectives.
6. Identify issues, problems, knowledge gaps and suggest solutions.
7. Identify steps in the processes.
8. Identify elements, characteristics, determinants and factors of the particular knowledge discussed in the text.
9. Locate and note information that answers specific questions.
10. Summarise, synthesise and paraphrase the reading points to form new thoughts.

Different strategies are used for different types of reading materials, reading aim, timing and difficulty of reading questions. However, developing comprehension begins with previewing and selecting suitable, appropriate and relevant material with the reading goal (the specific area of knowledge to learn) in mind. Asking questions before reading is able to create reading interest. Key words and author's notes in a text help to navigate the material. In addition, strategies such as predicting, assuming, inferring, comparing, deducing and synthesizing will build comprehension during reading. These strategies help readers to achieve reading goals. After reading, strategies such as summarizing, paraphrasing, rereading (a portion or the whole text), and reviewing, ensure the reader's comprehension.

Further discussion and reflection, and shared reading with others (especially those with a similar interest) help strengthen the reader's level of understanding. Additionally, visualisation and make connections between life experience subjects in the text will deepen the level of understanding and comprehension.

In summary, reading is a basis for good living by exposing and updating ourselves to new information and ideas, allowing self improvement, improving understanding, preparing us for action, widening our experience, developing tools of communication, nourishing the brain, and boosting imagination and creativity.

9 Managing Communication and Relationship

To the best of the author's knowledge, there is no specific guideline, mandatory rule or procedure to create the most effective interpersonal relations and communication. However, mutual understanding and general ideas (*rules of thumb*) as discussed in this book is believed sufficient to establish harmonious interpersonal relations and communication, especially between people with differing psychological, emotional, biological, situational, and cultural backgrounds, who have a range of identities, personality, and characteristics.

BARRIERS TO EFFECTIVE INTERPERSONAL RELATIONS AND COMMUNICATION

As discussed in Chapter three, there are several communication 'noises' which interrupt the completeness of interpersonal communication and relationship building. Foremost, language is seen as the most influential barrier to effective relations and communication within or across cultural boundaries. People who converse in a language with different linguistic characteristics to their own are likely to misinterpret the spoken message of the others. People may be influenced by differing perception, intention, focus, goal, *side-talking*, socio-cultural, and other biological and psychological 'noises' when engaging in interpersonal encounters. Besides, communication breakdown can occur due to abbreviation, simplification, mis-representation, interruption or modification of the original meaning in the process of passing the information from one to another. Furthermore, language confusion occurs when different words within the same group of language are used to convey the same meaning (i.e. different dialects). For example, comparing British English with American English, we find words such as petrol—gas, football—soccer, rugby—football, washroom—toilet and apartment—flat. Other barriers to effective communication and relations are discussed in the following section.

1. **Communication signals or clues.** There are tendencies for communication conflict due to dissimilarities or inconsistency of the communication signals or clues (symbols, words, languages or dialects) especially within or across cultural groups. People might interpret those communication clues differently from one cultural group to another. For example, showing five fingers to show a sign of 'talk to the hand' or 'denial' might be interpreted as 'good bye', 'give five', agreement or forgiveness by others from a different cognitive cultural group.

2. **Credibility.** Credibility is the quality, capability, or power to elicit trust and belief; to influence, inspire and convince; and to execute the meaning (ideas, perceptions or feelings) of the message. Thus, it is vital to ensure the source of credibility in writing or speaking is given by proper, precise and wise arrangement of words, sentences, phrases and tones. The credibility of the communication source can be questionable if the meaning of the message is unclear, incomplete or unknown; if it has double-standards or is propaganda, assuming the listener or receiver has a choice of accepting, rejecting or ignoring the message. For example, a gardener who talks about the formation of colour spectrum which is reflected by the condensed vapour on the leaves' surfaces in the morning may not be perceived as a trustworthy source as he is not the scientist. However, any knowledge or ideas come from non-expert in the field for the particular enquiry is perceived as public opinions or testimony (accordingly to their observation, perception, feeling or experience). Wanting credibility of the communication source

makes people take extra precautions to avoid "untrustworthy" materials and being skeptical. However, in the end, "Lies, in fact seemed to be remembered better than truths" (Hovland & Weiss, 1951: p.635).

3. **Social differences**. Reluctance to communicate, rejection, annoyance or distrust happens due to the different social status, background, credibility, time, goal, perception, feeling and intention between people. Some people who hold esteemed status will probably demand personal space or privacy. They would decry sharing the use of public facilities or other common accommodation with those whom they consider having a lower income, are uncivilised, are the rural under-developed, or unfortunate in other ways. They believe that with their higher status (hierarchy or ranking), title, level of income, education and the job, they should be given special treatment, accommodation or hospitality. People who are creating social distance or status try to retain respect, power, image, dominance, privilege, and security. They may also have racist sentiments or show ethnocentrism.

4. **Frame of references**. Different cultural groups have dissimilar sets of values, beliefs, norms and perceptions. Contrasting cultural references may create conflict or disagreement among people with regard to certain issues. For example in a cross-cultural business negotiation between Americans and Japanese, the Americans who required prompt responses (either acceptance or rejection) were not able to close the deal. This scenario happened because the Japanese associates nodded their heads to show understanding of the discussed point or negotiations, yet be in agreement of business deal. A frame of reference is developed from past experiences, propaganda flyers, clippings, advice (by family members, friends, partners, neighbours, colleagues or strangers) or personal experience of events, before making the decision react or respond to the message.

5. **Knowledge and skills**. Language is a medium to exchange knowledge, skill, perception, feeling and expectation. People

with lingua franca which are not English might experience difficulty with conversing in English due to the influence of their dialects, mother-tongue accents or slang. Of course, some biological or medical disabilities since birth, such as dyslexia and downs-syndrome also contribute to communication difficulties. Likewise, the type of sensory learning might also influence the effectiveness of interpersonal communication and relations. People are visual, auditory or kinaesthetic (VAK) in their cognitive preference, and must be treated accordingly.

a. Those who have **visual** cognitive domination (seeing) actively react to visible objects, pictures or demonstrations, and these determine their level of understanding of the message communicated. For example, they can only execute instructions to bake a cake after a physical demonstration is made, even if a completed recipe is given earlier. The communication is ineffective without visual materials to show or explain the meaning (ideas, feeling or perceptions) of the message.

b. People who have **auditory** cognitive domination (hearing) only actively react after listening to voices or sounds. A person might be unable to work effectively in a quiet environment or without proper audio instructions. For example, instructions to prepare a report or document from memos or letters (attached with a complete manual with pictures) are only executed after the task has been explained verbally.

c. A person who has **kinaesthetic** cognitive domination actively reacts to non-static visual or not monotonous audio. Five senses: sight (seeing), hearing (listening), smelling, feeling (touch), and tasting; cultivate a psychological and physical reaction especially with aids of audio-visual instructions. However, concentration is interrupted by unexpected or large amounts of audio (noises, voice or sound) or visual (movements).

There are difficulties with identifying, examining or getting to know the sensory domination of a person *impromptu* and without proper psychological testing. Hence, in order to create effective relations and communication, we must tackle the receivers' (audiences, viewers, listeners, clients, or customers) attention, and responses as expected: the prepared source needs to be appropriate, interesting, complete, precise, beautiful, colourful and creative audio-visually, using samples, supporting materials or aids for presentation or demonstration.

EFFECTIVE INTERPERSONAL RELATIONS AND COMMUNICATION

In managing interpersonal relations and achieving effective communication, consistency is needed in forming words or language (verbal or non-verbal). This ensures the meanings (ideas, feelings or perceptions) of messages are well-received and understandable. For instance, sufficient and appropriate communication knowledge and skills are vital to create harmony that will benefit the interpersonal interaction process. Hence, the communicators (senders and receivers, speakers and listeners, demonstrators or presenters and audiences) need to pay attention to several aspects to improve the effectiveness of interpersonal relations and communication. These will be discussed in the following section.

1. **Adjustment and adaptability.** People's understanding, acceptance, rejection, annoyance or ignorance of the communication processes are determined by many biological and situational factors such as: knowledge, skill, culture, academic background, expertise, and social status. Therefore, it is essential for a communicator to understand, and be sensitive to the character or personality of others, as well as factors like timing, location, materials used and reasons for communicating the message. In certain circumstances, there are unexpected mechanical difficulties, such as electricity shut-down, heat, smell, machines or equipment default, which interfere, jeopardize, break off, suspend, alter or shift communicators' attention and interrupt the communication process. Thus, communicators (senders, speakers, debaters, preachers or demonstrators) should be prepared to adjust to any consequences of interruption, effects of feedbacks or responses, and to maintain the momentum or credibility. For example, at a time audio-visual equipments (example, projector) are malfunctioning or are not available, a

backup-plan such as a printed handout is helpful to rescue the communication process.

2. **Psychological reaction. A** 'giving vs. taking' principle is essential to establish a mutual and beneficial relationship. Enrich 'giving' by involving love, patience, acceptance, acknowledgement, appreciation, passion, humility, excitement, and understanding. In contrast, try to reduce expectation of 'taking' such as envy, irritation, ignorance, annoyance, arrogance, scepticism, prejudice, anger, hate, fear and boredom. Thus, both parties who are involved in the interpersonal communication should be aware of the speaking and/or listening needs; respect the protocol; give space and time for reactions, feedback or responses; and show appropriate acceptance or rejection of the communicated message.

3. **Language and meaning**. People involved or participating in a communication process need to be aware of the usage of language and the meaning (ideas, feelings or perceptions) of the message. Different languages use similar words or phrases but they represent different meanings, especially in different cultural groups. For example, the word 'seronok' in the Malaysian Malay language means 'happy' but the same word could refer to 'having sex' in the Indonesian language. On the other hand, there are situations where the same words or phrases represent similar meanings in different languages. For example, 'bomba' mean fire-fighter in the Philippine Tagalog and Malaysian Malay language. However, the most vital element to establishing beneficial and effective interpersonal relations and communications is to avoid, as much as possible, writing or speaking the language that is insulting, immature, impropriate, sexist, racist, ethnocentric, or has double-meaning. Hence, appropriate knowledge and skills are required to regulate the written or spoken message, to avoid insulting or confusing the reader or listener.

4. **Speaking and listening skills.** In verbal communication, speaking and listening are two different but interdependent actions, to ensure interpersonal communication and relationship

effectiveness. A good or excellent speaker, debater or preacher is a person who is knowledgeable, credible, creative, has a sense of humour, shows appropriate verbal and non-verbal reactions, and is able to convince or persuade the listeners or audience about the talking points. On the other hand, active listening is a communication skill which requires a listener to be aware, focused and attentive. This enables him/her to take part in a communication session, give appropriate responses, and show appropriate verbal and non-verbal reactions.

5. **Credibility maintenance.** Credibility in communication is a crucial aspect as discussed in earlier sections (barriers to the effective interpersonal relations and communication). Thus, to ensure a beneficial and effective communication process, communicators, especially a source, speakers, debaters or preachers, need to develop, sustain or maintain the credibility of the message. Maintaining message credibility is by: acquiring appropriate speaking and writing skills; and using appropriate and effective supporting aids or materials. Moreover, in the Theory of Interpersonal Trust in the communication process as posited by Giffin (1967), 'trust' is a main source of credibility for effective interpersonal relations and communication. In creating highest acceptance of credibility, trust development is based on the receivers' (listeners' or audiences) past experiences, testimony or perception about the source's (speaker, debater, preacher or demonstrator) personality, expertise, reliability, intentions, activeness, personal attractiveness, attentiveness, passion, and the majority opinion or responses toward the messages.

6. **Sensitivity.** Sensitivity is an ability to understand and give appropriate reactions according to similarities or differences in the behaviours, ideas, feelings or perceptions. To avoid misconduct or communication break-down, the communicators are require to be sensitive to both parties, (senders and receivers, speakers and listeners, demonstrators or presenters and audiences) with perspectives on their level of understanding, background, socio-culture, reputation and interest. It is necessary for them to avoid "jumping to a conclusion", "judging a book by its cover", or

making personal judgments and assumptions towards the other's decisions, comments, complaints, ideas, feelings, perceptions, opinions, responses or reactions.

7. **Follow-up.** Incomplete communication process occurs due to unexpected feedback or lack of response. Therefore, it is essential for the source or senders to follow-up by rewriting, re-contacting or reminding the receiver about the given message. Request for feedback or responses must be given in the most polite, precise, appropriate channels and suitable forms, such as: a formal letter of reminder; or symbolic enquiries (social visits, festive season gifts or invitation to an event); or legal actions (summons). Appropriate selection of communication mode or channel could help to avoid irritation, ignorance, annoyance or distracting reactions.

8. **'Richness' of the communication media.** There are various types of communication medium that can be used as a vehicle to transport the message and create effective communication. Each communication medium has its own purpose, costs and benefits of the use.

    a. *Telephone:* verbal or non-verbal message are transferred or communicated using the in-ground phone lines, or cellular or satellite networks such as voice communication, Short Messaging System (SMS) and Multimedia Messaging System (MMS). Tele-marketing is a technique in which the business companies contact customers or prospective clients, promoting their products or services via phone conversation. In order to sustain mutual relationships, build a good rapport or corporate image, some companies offer a specific *toll-free* or *hotline* number to their call-centre in order to provide after-sales services and entertain any complaints, comments or provide technical assistance.

    b. *Fax:* transmits documents containing text and graphics over ordinary telephone line, but the sending and receiving messages have to use particular fax machines.

c. *Internet:* is an open communication network over the in-ground phone line (wired) or satellite communication technology. Registration and subscription to the cellular service provider is needed which incurs subscription fees. It also needs specific electric and electronic devices (personal computers, laptop, notebook, smart phone, modem, broadband), and has limited bandwidth (uploading and downloading capacity) or geographical service coverage. Moreover, Internet networks are exposed to technological attacks or hackers (spam, virus, worm, trojan) which harm the electronic devices. Internet is quick sources of knowledge. However, the Internet is exposing to the information violation and exploitation by irresponsible individual. For example, a burglar may use the Internet map to study about the geographical area before committing a crime. Thus, security precautions are important to safeguard the information by promoting 'website' membership and putting access password.

d. *Intranet:* is a closed organizational communication network over the internet or wired technology, but with limited accessibility (only within the organization internal communication network and used only among the organizational employees).

e. *Email:* gives instantaneous transmission of a message which is accessed by using electronic devices (personal computer, laptop, notebook, smart phone) with specific email accounts and websites through Internet networks such as Yahoo, Hotmail and Gmail.

f. *Instant messaging (IM):* describes computer network application for real-time communication or instant conversation by text, audio and/or visual interaction. For example, Yahoo Messenger, MSN, Tweeter, Google talk or Skype.

g. *Voice mail:* digitizes short spoken messages, transmitted over the network by a particular cellular service provider, stored on disc, retrieved later by the receiver, who hears the recorded voice message.

h. *Teleconferencing:* describes the interaction on a one-to-one basis or in group conferencing simultaneously with a real-time audio system, using an ordinary telephone or computer-to-computer network and conferencing software. Specific electronic devices are needed, and the communicators must be available at the same time for teleconferencing.

i. *Video-conferencing:* describes the one-to-one interaction or group conferencing simultaneously at different locations by using an audio-visual system over video screens. Similar to teleconferencing, specific electronic devices are needed and the communicators must be available at the same time.

j. *Broadcast:* the Internet, radio and television are the mediums to convey a message through wired or satellite communication signals which transfer the message from one location to another. With this technology, live broadcasting of, for example, a football match of the European League can be watched in real-time in different locations around the globe.

k. *Other printed media:* magazines or books are published with exclusive themes according to interests, hobbies, activities, jobs, culture and purposes. However, rapid and reliable accessibility to the Internet (by smart phone or electronic devices) has been replaced the functions of magazines, books and other printed reading material. Thus, new electronic forms of e-magazines or e-books are able to reach the targets (readers or viewers) faster, and are downloadable, more elaborate and interesting using audio-visual and multimedia presentations. Similarly, for a short radius of promotions or announcements, booklet, monograph, door hanger, book marker, billboard, banner, bunting and flyer are probably the right mediums to use. However, they have a limited range for the large amount of information, are time-consuming and incur a high financial cost for materials, printings and distribution.

Media as a powerful communication medium helps uphold knowledge and information expansion and enhancement. The messages convey in the media could be the act as judiciary, economist, politicians, educators, informers, marketers and so forth. Hence, selecting the right media is crucial to ensure that the messages reach the right target audience.

In addition to the valuable aspects of interpersonal relationships established as above, Newsom, Turk and Kruckeberg (2000) posited the 7 C's formula for creating effective interpersonal relations, communication and mutual public relations. These include:

1. *Credibility*: Is a climate of belief and trust which reflect a desire to serve the receiver. The receiver must have confidence in the sender's message after taking into consideration the sender's image, reputation, background, performance, work establishment and personality.

2. *Context*: Is where communication takes place. It includes the location and surrounding environment.

3. *Content*: This deals with the meaning of the message being conveyed and may involve the problem of understanding or estimating the impact of the message. In other words, the message must have meaning relevant to the receiver. It should therefore be advisable for the speaker to know the background, intentions and interest of the targeted audience.

4. *Clarity*: Making the message clear, simple and understandable. The message information must be sufficient and thoroughly supported with relevant examples, and data.

5. *Continuity and Consistency*: As the process of communication becomes on-going, reasonable repetition with variation is required to achieve a significantly understood, accepted and remembered message.

6. *Channel*: Describes the vehicle or ways to communicate. They must be relevant and suitable to the message and audience.

7. *Capability*: This means the audience ability to handle the message, their expectation and needs for the message. It depends on the audience's backgrounds, habits and interests.

INTERPERSONAL COMMUNICATION AND RELATIONSHIP CYCLE MODEL

At the centre of the interpersonal communication and relationship issue is the notion that sufficient and appropriate understanding, knowledge and skills is crucial to establish effective and beneficial interpersonal relationships. In an organization, employees' commitment and intention to stay are dependent on the leader's communicative strategies (Mayfield & Mayfield, 2002, 2007). Moreover, the sender needs to initiate effective relations and communication strategies, techniques and tactics. Delineated from the discussion as above, we would like to propose an interaction cycle model known as the Interpersonal communication and relationship (IRC) Cycle Model. IRC Cycle Model posits the interaction system in order to establish and sustain interpersonal relations as shown in Figure 9.1. There are four stages in the IRC cycle which indicate actions that should take place in order to ensure complete and beneficial communication establishment and interpersonal relations.

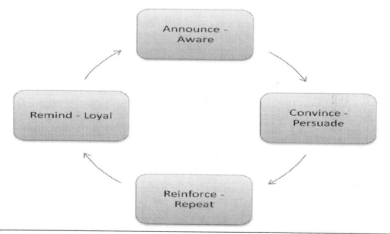

Figure 9.1: IRC Cycle Model
Source: Author

Stage 1: *Announce—Aware*

Initially, the communication source (sender, speaker, debater, preacher) has a meaning (ideas, feelings or intentions) of the message to initiate or announce to the targeted receiver (listener or audience), expecting to receive responses, feedback or actions in return. However, before transmitting the message, a person (sender) probably has experience in conducting, receiving or sending similar message, instructions, requests, orders, directions or announcements. New messages are composed in order to correct, enhance, expand or extend the knowledge and information to others. It is a signal for the source to request for reactions, support, sympathy, involvement, cooperation or interest from the others (such as subordinates or colleagues) and initiate the communication process. At this early stage of the IRC cycle, the messages are sent to create some awareness or attention in the receivers and to invite or request their response. For example, a commercial advertisement is made to elicit purchases from customers. Thus, various choices of vehicles (methods, mediums, channels, forums or forms) of communication (verbal or non-verbal) can be chosen to convey the message, notification or announcement and create public awareness. Selecting appropriate, cost efficient communication vehicles is a critical decision to make in order to ensure the messages are transferable, reach the right target and achieve the ultimate goal (such as work done, placing orders, starting or increasing sales or profit).

A creative, innovative, simple but precise and complete message, supported by interesting presentation, determines the speed and effectiveness of the message. In human psychology, the message is basically understood, and stimulated brain reactions are stimulated by a proper combination of colours, pictures and 'middle spot' or focus of a message. This is known as concept mapping. A creative stimulation of the human brain, using colours, pictures and middle spot, is able to achieve expected awareness, attention and reactions. In other words, differences, innovation and creativity are the weapons to create awareness, to impress audiences, and to attract their willingness to respond. However, as required by the public relations regulations in Malaysia, mass media communication is guided by specific journalism or communication rules and regulations, especially with regard to multiethnic issues, national defence and religious concerns.

Stage 2: *Convince—Persuade*

Upon receiving a communication signal (news alert, advertisement, notification, or announcement), the message receivers (listeners, audience, or customers) have the right to react, respond, give required feedback, accept, reject, or ignore the message. The pace of response depends on the receivers' biological, physical, psychological, organizational, situational or socio-cultural factors such as: sense of urgency; impotency of the message; implications of effect after feedback or responses are given; level of understanding or complexity of the message; reliability or availability of the response channels; and timing, distance and cost involved. Therefore, to obtain the number, amount, speed, quantity and quality of the feedback or responses as required or expected, it is important that the senders properly craft, write, arrange, design or encode the meanings (ideas, feeling or perceptions) of the message into simple, precise, persuasive, convincing, understandable and interesting form. Persuasive messages are written or spoken with proper and appropriate selection or use of words and phrases, grammar, order, language, dialect and tone. In addition, the impact of the message is enhanced through the using of appropriate presentation aids such as audio-visual multimedia, design and colour. As discussed in earlier sections, the credibility of the source (image, reputation, experience, expertise and background) is vital to ensure that receiver believe the message and give prompt and appropriate responses as expected or required.

Likewise, innovative, creative, proactive and persuasive forms of the verbal or non-verbal communication methods; techniques or tactics (letters, memos, flyers, bunting, booklets, monographs, adverts, phone calls, visits (courtesy visit to the office or home); or samples, gifts, parties, seminars, conferences or contests are arranged, prepared or given in order to gain immediate action, responses or feedback from the receivers. In addition, gifts like book-marks, key chains, coupons (for shopping, cinema or food), money back guarantees, cash, or other tokens of appreciation are offered to persuade or encourage volume of responses.

Stage 3: *Reinforce—Repeat*

There are messages which do not require a prompt reply, feedback or response, such as an announcement or advertisement (for example, launching a new product; change of location information; new store opening; forthcoming events; submissions; publications; payments due; or obituaries). Therefore, a follow-up, friendly reminder, repetition of the advertisement, announcement or news alert is able to ensure the receivers are aware, remember, and respond sometime in the future. In spite of the existence of verbal, written or other formal forms of communication to establish mutual relations, other non-verbal types of communication are able to reinforce the message. However, appropriate facial expression, body movement and gesture, and physical contact should be expressed with caution in order to avoid any misinterpretation, rejection, ignorance or annoyance by the messages' receiver. In addition, in order to improve interpersonal relationships or response time, senders could offer appropriate communication aids (such as return envelopes with payable postage stamps, forms to complete, templates, maps, contact details) and tokens of appreciation (perks, gifts, or souvenirs).

However, there are cases where feedback is delayed or non-existent, or the receivers disappear or refuse to give responses as required, instructed or expected. Thus, appropriate and procedural legal actions can be taken, such as: calling emergency corporate meetings; issuing bankruptcy declarations or a writ of summons; starting contempt of court proceedings; or applying for arbitration. On the other side, to protect receivers from exploitation or business fraud, it is important the receivers (especially consumers) are aware of their consumer rights, obligations and protection. Therefore, receivers are advised to read carefully and understand stated or written information in letters, memos, agreements, adverts, product labels (related information such as contents of the products, expiry dates, and producers), rules and regulations, terms and conditions, and instructions or orders, and other written material.

Stage 4: *Remind—Loyal*

In sales and marketing, the idea of *after sales service* is to make the customers feel that the product they purchased is worth buying. The same concept is applied to general interpersonal communication and relationship to ensure beneficial, continuous and long-term relationships. Appreciation or acknowledgement is a technique to show acceptance and thanks by communicators. It is expressed through appropriate channels, remembrances or reward systems such as salary or wage increments, yearly bonuses, free trips, samples, discounts, rebates, priority and other loyalty membership programs.

In addition, we do believe in the word-of-mouth effect of spreading information, news, recommendations, compliments, testimony, references, complaints or traumatic experiences. Hence, people may refer, forward or recommend the products, services, place or personnel to their friends, colleagues, families or contacts, and vice versa for negative images (such as accidents or fraud, profit lost, image damage). Although regular, repetitive or frequent reminders or advertisements incur substantial costs (for time, location, printing, broadcasting or distribution) the sender will gain long-term commercial benefits (such as cost efficiency or economies of scale) and client loyalty or continuous purchasing. For example, almost everybody, regardless of their demographic characteristic, knows, has heard of or recognized global brands such as McDonald, KFC, Pizza Hut, Coca-cola and Pepsi. Familiarity with such global brands has been established by the companies continuously and frequently advertising their name and products in prime network time to staple their brand into the users' mind. The announcements of new products, promotions, events, seasonal greetings, regular products or services are made through various communication media and channels (printed or broadcast channels). Besides, some Multinational Corporations (MNCs) based in Malaysia such as PETRONAS, Shell and Tenaga National Berhad (TNB) also advertised products, services or convey social messages in their seasonal or festive advertisements in Malaysian mass media, to show their concern or corporate social responsibility. It is clear that repetitive strategy is an effective way to establish loyalty, mutual and beneficial relationships.

Finally, after reaching stage four of the IRC Cycle, it may revolve back to stage one, and the process is repeated for another new message, interaction, event or set of receivers (listeners, audience, customers, clients). An IRC cycle continues until the messages, promotions or advertisements either achieve the saturation level (maximum sales or profits obtained or declining), become out-of-date, are rejected or do not meet the stated or expected goals.

10 Conflict Management

Conflict is a disagreement in a communication and relationship. Conflict happens within an individual (intrapersonal) or between two or more people (interpersonal). It can take the form of false or default information (informational) or an ineffective result or outcome (decisional). Disagreement happens when people see and perceive things differently due to one or more of the following: dissimilar frames of references, knowledge and skills, understanding, culture (values, beliefs, and norms), experiences, level of maturity, personalities, perceptions and feelings, thinking styles, status, goals, approaches, ideological and philosophical references, emotional and other socio-cultural, economic and political backgrounds. Besides, conflict within an organization may occur due to biases, conflict of interest, rules and regulations, leadership styles, performance expectations and assessment, lack of resources, cooperation and involvement, and remuneration or welfare being incompatible with workloads. To simplify: disagreement or conflict occurs as people are vary in their *affective* (feeling, emotion, soul), *cognitive* (mind, perception, personality, knowledge) and *behavioural* (skills, actions) systems. Thus, finding appropriate meeting points of the affective, cognitive and behavioural aspects are important to dissolve the disagreement. Inappropriate solutions or unsolved problems may create conflicts ranging from annoyance to a quarrel or fight; or from ignorance to annoyance, separation or divorce. Additionally, a political conflict may cause wider damage such as executions, rebellion and war. Hence, it is vital for us to identify any possible causes of conflict and propose appropriate solutions to these problems.

CONFLICT IN COMMON

A conflict occurs with the existence of three distinct elements, including power, demand and worth.

- **Power.** Is an ability to execute or enforce ideas which may create a conflict. People may have different psychological or physical ability to overcome the differences depending on the critical level of the problems. Inappropriate use of power may cause exploitation, quarrel, rebellion, or war.
- **Demand.** Is created by the need to obtain fairness or justice, close the status gap or socio-cultural differences, and fulfil the personal goals, needs and wants in interpersonal relationship building. Conflict occurs due to inequality or unexpected outcome, feedback or result from the particular communication or relationships.
- **Worth.** Unequal or unexpected benefits or outcomes of works create conflict in order to fulfil the need or gain what we want. For example, with so much effort given day and night to achieve targeted sales, we would expect to be nominated for an excellent reward for that particular year. If somebody else gets the reward, we conflict with the superior over his/her bias, ignorance, or unequal performance assessment.

Conflict is usually seen as a negative aspect in a relationship, to be avoided. However, conflict may bring both positive and negative effects. Positive effects of conflict are that it:

- Stimulates new research activities, ideas, facts, creations, solutions, methods, techniques, knowledge, skills, suggestions or resolutions.
- Increase individual or group cohesion, understanding, knowledge, productivity, creativity, initiative and performance.

- Demonstrates a stand of opinions, philosophy, ideology, showing bravery, power or ability.
- Expands networking, connections or social support.
- Establishes new relationships or direction of communication.
- Break barriers or red tape and simplifies rules and procedures.
- Changes or restructures the chain of command or line of authority.
- Creates an opportunity for new projects, jobs or recruitment.
- Improves the works systems and quality of output.
- Replace old systems, methods, techniques or tactics with new systems that are more accurate, cost effective and reliable.

On the other hand, negative effects of the conflict are that it:

- Hinders or restricts freedom or smooth processes.
- Expands costs and quantity of resources, and time of job completion.
- Jeopardizes or reduces the performance, quality, productivity, talent, morale, motivation, effectiveness and functionality of the system.
- Causes reformation, re-engineering, restructure or relocation of the project or system.
- Break the communication channel and relationships.
- Causes inappropriate competition and in-fighting.
- Increases tensions and stress.
- Breaks the team into small groups, or gangs.
- Establishes unnecessary propaganda, accusations or grudges.
- Affects property, information or secrecy disclosure.

Hence, people might access, evaluate and oversee the conflict for both positive and negative effect. The following sections will discuss the conflict from the different perspectives of intrapersonal, interpersonal, informational and decisional.

INTRAPERSONAL CONFLICT

Intrapersonal communication is a self concept which involves self-awareness, self-sensitivity, self-discrepancy, self-development and so forth. Intrapersonal conflict involves a communication process within a person of self-talking, back-head whispering or imagination or day-dreaming. Intrapersonal or self conflict occurs when we internally argue with ourselves about something, or are unable to make a wise decision especially for him/herself, or are forced to make a decision for somebody else. This results in confusion, 'black-out', depression or stress. The conflict may develop out of self thoughts, ideas, emotions, plans, values, beliefs, knowledge, skills or readiness. Unorganized intrapersonal conflict may cause harm to the health, leading to headaches, fever, irrational action, emotional instability (crying, laughing, mumbling, withdrawing) or mental disorder (suicide, madness). Examples of intrapersonal conflict are:

- Someone who is dieting having to choose either to eat or keep fasting after being invited for a lunch-time party.
- A teenager conflicting either to stay at home studying or follow friends to the cinema, when the final examinations are around the corner.
- A lady confused when having to choose a matching colour of attires (blouses, shirts, shoes and handbag) before going out for hi-tea.
- A person knowing somebody's secret wondering whether to keep the secret or tell somebody else.
- A person spending money for something unplanned such as buying new shoes, and so forth.

Hence, intrapersonal conflict is perceived as a psychological interruption or disorder which affects the effectiveness of decision making, daily activities, routines, emotional stability, friendships or relationships. Internal disorder is not always easy to identify until the existence of discomfort, mood swings or depression. Intrapersonal conflict occurs when we need to choose between two or more goals, events or options. Some of us lack the internal strength to handle stress, pressure or conflict and thus, referring to someone, especially professionals, for advice, guidance or counselling is a solution for intrapersonal conflict management.

INTERPERSONAL CONFLICT

Interpersonal is a relationship established between two or more people, verbal or nonverbal, physically, mentally or visually connected. Differences in affective, cognitive and behavioural aspects create disagreement or conflict with somebody else or different groups, teams, associations, societies or nations. Different level of conflict, seriousness and expectations occur between couples, friends, co-workers, siblings, spouses, partners, roommates, neighbours, cultural groups, regions or nations. People may respond or give feedback to the questions, enquiry or disagreement in different ways dependent on his/her knowledge, emotional and physical wellbeing, personal feelings, socio-cultural background (values, norms, and beliefs), goals, understanding, complexity or urgency of the messages. Hence, interpersonal conflict occurs, when responses are misinterpreted, misrepresented, misunderstood, irresponsible, exaggerated totally wrong or unexpected. Several types of interpersonal conflict are:

1. **Emotional**. Emotion is an affective element which determines the feeling or mood toward response. Emotions may be hidden or become salient factors that influence the communication conflict and relationships tensions. Being angry, sad, disgusted or annoyed are emotions which add to the effect of disagreement, conflict or dispute. Thus, we need to control the emotional effect before decision making or responding to the disagreement, to avoid unexpected incidents (such as fights, quarrels or rebellions).

2. **Opinions**. Difference in knowledge, skills, experience, age, gender, frame of references, status, expectation, interests, feelings, goals, life styles, origin, hierarchy or socio-cultural background (ethnicity, race, religion, possessions) makes different people see things differently and differ in opinion. Differences in opinion could result in healthy relationships which create creativity and diverse solutions to problems. However, different opinions due to the social status, ranking or hierarchy cause relationship conflict when perceived as challenges, frustrations, annoyances, ignorance or denial. Hence, communicating appropriate thoughts with reasonable justification, facts and data are able to solve the conflict.

3. **Values** are the standards by which we perceive things as right or wrong, just or unjust, and appropriate or inappropriate. Values are created through socio-cultural composition, origin, family, friends or society, which all influence our judgement, justifications and rationality. For example, for rich people, one cent is considered nothing, but for poor people, it may make a large difference. They put a different value on money. Differently perceived values challenge our level of understanding, acceptance or rejection which triggers problems in finding an interception point of agreement. Thus, values influence communication and relationship building.

4. **Belief** is an element that we trust or perceive as correct, right or appropriate. Similar to values, socio-cultural composition, origin, family, friends and society all shape our belief systems. Beliefs guide or shape certain behaviour, decisions or ways of communication and relationship creation pertaining religion, politics, history and many things in life. For example, Islamic teaching and belief that living together before being legally married is a sin and may cause social problems. There are some natural phenomena (known as an anomaly effect) that influence human belief systems, such as less people engaging in the stock market during a raining season. This belief is based on experience although there are few facts to support the belief. Belief systems ultimately become part of conversation and communication processes. They influence the quality of the decision, response or conflict resolution. Differences in belief trigger interpersonal conflict, especially when encountering those holding a traditional or conventional belief, or those closed-minded to new perspectives, changes, opinions or understandings. Hence, respect, collaboration and ability to compromise are the key to avoid interpersonal conflict due to differences in belief.

5. **Personality.** Personality is a combination of individual qualities that form a personal distinctive character. Different ways-of-being or presentation of self appears as one of the causes of interpersonal communication and relationship conflict. Individual personality is developed based on socio-cultural

background, family, society and surround living environment. Bandura (1977) in his Social Learning Theory emphasizes the personality is build up through imitation, observational and modelling learning the behaviours, attitudes, and emotional reactions of others. The quality of decision or behaviour is affected by different types of individual personality.

Personality conflict occurs when two or more people encounter incompatibility in their characters, perspectives, attitudes, approaches and styles. The personality also influences a person's attitude or traits which affect the quality of interactions, communication and relationships. In particular, the presentation of the message may cause the interpersonal communication and relationship conflict rather than the personality. Inappropriate presentation, interpretation or understanding of personality appearance creates a gap or distance between people. According to Costa and McCrea (1976), there are five types of common personality (known as the Big Five personalities) as follows:

a. *Agreeableness.* A character that makes a person has a tendency to be compassionate, cooperative and tolerant, with a great amount of trust, kindness, affection and other sociological behaviour.

b. *Conscientiousness.* A character when a person shows self-discipline, is eager for success and aims for achievement, is well organized and plans actions, is dependable, self-controlled and goal-oriented. Those high in conscientiousness show strong allegiance to decisions or goals.

c. *Extraversion.* A character that shows an outgoing or energetic type of person, who has positive emotions, assertiveness, sociability, and emotional expressiveness. They are talkative and friendly. Those high in extraversion are extrovert types of people.

d. *Neuroticism.* A type of character in which a person is sensitive, nervous, emotionally unstable, dependent, anxious, moody, irritable and sad. Appropriate social support is able to help a neurotic feel more secure and protected, confident and brave. In contrast to the extravert, those high in neuroticism are introvert types of people.

e. ***Openness.*** A person with this type of character is highly inventive or curious, which creates creativity, initiative, a spirit of adventure, imagination and keen insight. They have a broad range of interests, a variety of experiences, and the ability to create something unusual or find new ways of doing things.

Hence, appropriate interpersonal skills, understanding and flexibility are required to understand and communicate with these very different types of individual personality. Besides, assigning tasks to people accordingly to their personality could make use the differences for group or team benefits. For example, a person with high in openness is suitable for public relation jobs, and those high in agreeableness could be attentive leader.

DECISIONAL CONFLICT

Every second in life we need to make a decision. From the simplest decision, such as what colour of t-shirt to wear, to making a difficult decision such as either separation or divorce to solve a marriage conflict. Decisional conflict occurs due to the uncertainty of feelings, perceptions and understanding about courses of action to take when there are several options to choose. For example, a couple may have received RM 100,000 from the return of a shared investment. The husband wants to reinvest the monies into a new portfolio investment but the wife planned to spend it on her dream vacation to South Island of New Zealand. Hence, the decision to make is either to reinvest the monies or spend it on a vacation. A decisional conflict may involve cost, risk and challenges which may have positive results such as happiness, satisfaction, a mutual and beneficial relationship, profit, and peace; or negative outcomes such as loss, regret, bankruptcy, prison, quarrel, rebellion, disappointment, separation, relationship break-down or more stress. Every decision has a unique character, causes, action and effect. Thus, it is important for a responsible person to make a decision that is rational and has a wide perspective to foresee cause-and-effect of the decision. Support, advice, guidance, using standard operating procedure, manuals and other reading materials can be referred to in order to make wise decision.

INFORMATIONAL CONFLICT

Information is messages (ideas, feelings, perceptions), facts, figures, drawing or sketches which convey signals or clues to produce, change, correct or improve something (statics, concrete or flexible behaviours). Informational conflict occurs when the messages are nonexistent, incomplete, conveyed to the wrong person, hidden, manipulated, misrepresented or interpreted differently. Informational conflict occurs due to the person's level of understanding and acceptance, norms, values, beliefs and other internal or external influences. For example, a couple decides to use half of the monies received from their shared investment return for a vacation in the South Island of New Zealand. However, two travel agencies contacted give different information or travel packages (including itinerary, air fare and in-ground costs) to the couple. This causes further conflict of selection, timing and value-for-money.

A different magnitude of informational acceptance, interpretation and intention may cause a *conflict of interest* which may result in: problems remaining unsolved; a change of status-quo or standard; further debate, meeting or discussion; postponements, quarrels, disagreements or fighting. Conflict of interest occurs when people have different goals and intentions regarding the outcomes or effects of the events, activities or decisions. In addition, the problems may arise due to the perceptions, values, norms, beliefs, envy or grudges of the other people involved. For example, a job interviewer has conflict as one of the candidates is his wife.

In addition, the highest level of informational conflict may happen internally or within the organization which is known as *insider trading*. Insider trading or white-collar crime occurs when the internal members of the organization (probably officer-in-charge, executives, board of directors) misuse the information for their personal benefit or profit. For example, a company plans to launch new products to the public in May. In March after the board meeting, an executive buys a huge number of that company's shares, believing the stock price will increase at the time of the products' launching.

Therefore, appropriate assessment, evaluation, justification, judgement, audit, disclosure, procedures, protocol, reports and informational systems help to manage the information properly, using the right channel and reaching the right recipient.

CONFLICT MANAGEMENT STRATEGIES AND STYLES

Interpersonal conflict may cause damage to image, trust, reputation, credibility and relationships. Thus, appropriate solutions to the conflict should be understood and properly managed. According to Edward De Bono (De Bono, 1985), four ways to deal with conflict situations are:

- **Design.** A cause-and-effect of the conflict can be designed to discover the sources of the conflict, points of disagreement, its effect and consequences, and possible solutions to the problem. In designing the conflict, written, drawing or sketching techniques, such as mind mapping or a fish diagram, are effective tools to unfold any shortcoming or barriers to the problem.

- **Fight.** In certain circumstances which influence social status or hierarchy, job position (superior—subordinate, employer—employee), power, ego, image, credibility, performance and/or reputations, people strive to hold and defend the stance, standard, decision, opinion, work or relationship during an interpersonal conflict (fight, quarrel, jurisdiction, investigation, interrogation). Hence, in confronting or solving conflicts, a person needs to back his view with concrete evidence, facts, figures, support, and justification in order to prove his case. However, fight is not a professional way to solve conflict and could jeopardize relationship.

- **Negotiate.** Negotiation is a wise and most professional way to solve interpersonal conflict. People need to find the best time (without any emotional interference) meet and discuss possible solutions to the problem. The use of intermediaries or third parties (professionals, counsellors or superiors) is sometimes able to solve a critical problem between two or more conflicting people, groups or parties. Negotiations are a suitable process to figure out any barriers to the relationships; deal with the cost, benefits and possible consequences of the solution of the problem; and reach points of agreement and understanding. In an effective negotiation, people need to compromise to share any possible cost and benefits, and collaborate appropriately.

- **Solve the problem.** Other than negotiations or collaboration, people need to make corrections, replacements, or improvements to the issues or the problems. Some steps in problem solving include:

1. *Identify the issues that caused the conflict.* Issues that cause the difficulties or discomfort are the point to ponder. For example, a husband has a mistress or is having an affair with another woman.

2. *List possible changes to the usual events.* It is possible to identify the changes, signals, barriers or events that cause the problem. For example, a husband coming home late from work, who is always either silent, or makes cold conversation; has bitter responses in intimate or sexual relations; and gives reasons for going out.

3. *Identify the conflict.* A disagreement or unpleasant thought, feeling or perception between two or more people. For example, a quarrel between husband and wife even about unimportant things, such as not fastening properly the kitchen basin pipe.

4. *Realize the problems.* Before pointing out the cause of the problem to others, we need to be honest about any possibility that we ourselves are a starter or trigger to the problem. For example, a couple (either wife or husband, or both) after marriage may not be taking care of him/ herself (look, dress, size or health), or be too demanding, or fail to satisfy intimate or sexual needs or relations, or start complaining about the foods, cleanliness, appearances, happiness or love.

5. *List the choices of solutions.* Both conflicting parties should always welcome discussing and compromising the solutions. Active listening skills, brainstorming (asking for comments and suggestions), benchmarking (comparing or following the solution by other people, groups or

organisations) or ice-breaking (an informal session to know and understand the background or personality of the other) are examples of techniques to identify possible problems or solve conflicts. For example, asking for forgiveness, offering help, support, correction or replacement, or referring to third parties such as professional counsellors, parents or friends for advice, guidance, help and support.

6. ***Action taken and feedback.*** Before any actions are taken, both parties need to negotiate the solutions to avoid bigger problems, from any party. The agreements to the solutions of the problem are implemented must be executed as planned. In the process of managing the conflict, it is important for the conflicting parties to stay put and focus on the agreed solutions and control any interruption that may cause greater conflict. Importantly, characteristics like being calm, patient, trusting and respectful have a positive emotional and psychological effect to dissolve the conflict. Along the conflict solving process, feedback or responses work to identify possible room for improvement or avoid the conflict being repeated in the future.

Strategies of Conflict Management

Every conflict is unique, depending on its intensity, seriousness, and sources of conflict, effect or consequences of the result and people who are involved. Kenneth Thomas and Ralph Kilmann (Kilmann & Thomas, 1977; Thomas & Kilmann, 1974) suggest five styles or strategies to properly manage conflict. This is known as Thomas-Kilmann Conflict Mode Instrument (TKI).

1. ***Competing.*** People who stay firm to their opinion, right or decision will expect and ensure the other will follow, obey or listen and probably deny any objection or rejection. Competing strategy is used by selfish or dictator personalities who create a *win/lose* situation drawn from his/her position of power, ranking, status or hierarchy. This condition will leave others feeling dissatisfied, bruised, resentful, exploited or denied. However, with proper, solid, and trustworthy evidence, a strong personality,

knowledge, skills, influence and expertise, a person may take charge, lead, convince, persuade or enforce the decision. Besides, in certain circumstances of urgency, critical, fast action is needed or expected, or worse scenarios may take effect.

2. *Collaborating.* A democratic strategy in which a person tries to satisfy the needs of all people involved and agrees to the decision and its effect and consequences. Although a conflict has harmed the communication process, collaboration may save the relationship. Collaborating is a *win/win* situation when every conflicting person is involved with their viewpoints, ideas, suggestions and opinions acknowledged and incorporated in the conflict-solving. In order to establish a beneficial collaborating strategy, an appropriate negotiation process and high level of trust, understanding, responsibility, cooperation and involvement is required.

3. *Compromising.* Happens when one or both parties are willing to lose something to ensure the conflict is resolved and the others are satisfied. Compromising avoids the worst effects of conflict by accepting and considering other people's opinions, ideas, suggestions and feelings by offering trust or admitted the error. In a group, every person is expected to give up something, but somebody may take the opportunity to exploit the trust of the others. Compromising is a situation of *win-some/lose-some,* useful when the cost or effect of conflict is higher than values of friendship or possible consequences in the future. The main goal in compromising strategy is to resolve a conflict, albeit with some losses (for example, of property, satisfaction, respect, trust or friendship).

4. *Accommodating.* An accommodating strategy indicates the willingness of a person to fulfil the needs or satisfaction of the others to ensure the conflict is resolved. Accommodating strategy is applied when a person has strong back-up from total damage or loss. A person who is highly cooperative may, by surrendering the position, create a *lose/win* situation. In a conflict, the effect and cost of conflict may be high which

makes the accommodating strategy worthwhile for peace and harmonious outcomes. The 'winning' people might exploit the trust and kindness of the accommodator, which may damage the relationship. The accommodating strategy is beneficial when a person (accommodator) realises the conflict happened because of his/her mistake, or he/she cannot win the battle, or it is not appropriate to fight due to respect, or the issue is not important; or having other alternatives available.

5. ***Avoiding***. Some people evade the conflict completely. Such style typically concerns controversial issues, accepts the default decision, and keeps silent to maintain image or credibility. This conflict solution is questionable, sidestepping, postponing or delaying the problem, with a *lose/lose* situation being created. Avoiding strategy is applicable when the cost of conflict or pressure is too high, winning is impossible, the controversy is trivial, or there is somebody in a better position to resolve the conflict. Besides, avoiding is a correct strategy when: the position, power, responsibility or authority of a person has been denied; been forced to do so (to avoid or keep in silent by the court order); is protected or backed by law or somebody else; or has no chance to be involved or voice their ideas, feelings, opinions, perceptions or suggestions.

To conclude, conflict resolution depends on the participants' ability, maturity, emotional stability, rationality, personality, and credibility; their positions, status, hierarchy, ranking, power, and responsibilities; the costs and benefits of conflict resolution; the timing, situations, and possibly socio-cultural influences. There is no single right strategy to solve conflict, and choosing the right strategy depends on the needs, nature of the conflict and worth of interpersonal communication and relationships.

11 Conclusion

Communication is a method of establishing interpersonal relationships. Appropriate communication can ensure the creation of human chemistry for beneficial and mutual relationships. Effective communication is established by a completed process of message exchange using appropriate strategy, techniques and tactics. Effective or successful communications result in goal accomplishment and achievement, such as: economies of scale in business; work done as required or expected; gaining people's respect, trust, obedience, loyalty; avoiding or minimizing mistakes; and enhancing the effectiveness of relationships. However, misunderstanding, misinterpretation and intercultural difficulties may happen due to: disorganization or unexpected communications barriers; and differences in personality, mind-set, frame of references or socio-cultural background. To recap a quote by Ralph Waldo Emerson in the beginning of this book, most of the ideas outlined are a set of soft skills or methods to create mutual interpersonal relations and communication. Figure 7 summarizes Emerson's basic principles for establishing an effective interpersonal relationship and communication process. According to Emerson (2010), there are nine basic principles of effective relations and communication building:

1. **Treat each other with respect.** Respect is the science of appreciating, acknowledging and recognizing other people's personality, space, privacy, personal references, ideas, comments, suggestions, complaints, needs, wants and opinions. It is harmful to interpersonal relations if a person condemns, *judges a book by its cover*, jumps to a conclusion, points out other people's mistakes, accuses without any solid evidence or justification, or is ignorant or annoying. Nonetheless, as human beings, we need to be firm, keep our self-respect and rights, morale, image and dignity from being cheated or humiliated, especially in public. Therefore, it is important to minimize or avoid inappropriate behaviour, such as scepticism, racism, ethnocentrism (thinking one's own culture is greater than the others) or social desirability (doing good just to please people). Before dealing with the other, we need to acquire sufficient knowledge about the history of their culture (to explain their ways of behaving), personality or family background, track record of their past performances, experiences or trustable testimony. For example, historically, Arabs are known as fighters by Malayans. Thus, their communication approach is perceived as being harsher than Malay.

2. **Do not interrupt the conversation inappropriately, give other people personal space and permit other people to contribute (ideas, comments or suggestions).** In group discussions, team works, meetings, interviews, conversations, and negotiations; or even in disputes, fights or quarrels, the grouchiest person only shows his/her own stupidity or unprofessionalism as a result of uncivilised behaviour (zero knowledge about appropriate manners, rules and procedures or protocols). Hence, the professional way is by asking permission to interrupt, to acknowledge, praise or greet accordingly, to write formal letters, welcoming feedbacks or responses, by suggesting or giving justifications with sufficient evidence (samples, statistics or citations), and by learning the particular organization or events' protocols, acquiring knowledge and skills (such as table manners, records or documents preparation, speaking and listening). Besides, appropriate leaderships skills are vital to ensure the chain of command or line of authority is respected, and information

flows to the right channel. In addition, a conducive and peaceful surrounding, green environment or suitable *Feng Shui* is an element that could sustain a relaxing and effective workspace, for conflict resolution.

3. **Have a right to pass or do nothing rather that feel threatened and harm the relationship.** In certain circumstances, situations or events where people fail or are unable to establish expected relationships, gain profits or benefits, feedback or responses, mutual understanding, agreement, decisions or solutions, it is possible for them to find alternatives to solve the problem. Some reformations of solutions to the communication problems include: change of medias or communication channel; renegotiations; time extension (for work completion, repairing, rewriting, reinvestigating, collecting additional information, evidence or support); reviewing the needs, declarations, rules and procedures, terms and conditions, protocols; referring to or asking for advice from trustees (spouse, partners, friends, family, advisors, consultants, a particular public authority); or using mediators (third parties). The use of legal action (court jurisdictions) by writ of summons to solve a critical conflict incurs high costs, is time-consuming, and may cause damage to image, credibility or reputation. White-collar crimes could jeopardize the interpersonal relationship. White-collar crimes include: such as criminal misappropriation; *insider trading*; unauthorised transactions; or instigation that may harm the national security, sovereignty or sensitivity; human trafficking; criminal breach of trust; smuggling; abuses and corruption, which can result in heavy fines or compensations, expulsions, executions and/or imprisonments; enforced under the Malaysian criminal code. Besides, doing nothing, keeping quiet or in ignorance shows a sign of disagreements, rejections or lack of interest which in certain circumstances is able to avoid conflict.

4. **Do not volunteer others and recognise people's right to choose.** Every human has personal identity, intentions, expectations, interests, expertise, personality, knowledge, skills or preferences. The reasons people commit into a communication

are for self benefit, advancement, promotion or wealth, organization or business goal, and social, religious or national responsibility. Therefore, it is dangerous, unethical, inappropriate and ineffective to ask or volunteer others (especially those who are unfamiliar, non-expert or unpaid) to represent ourselves or the communication sources in decision making or communicating the message. The possible dangers in volunteer others include: message exploitation, miscommunication, misinterpretation, misconduct, conflict-of-interest or bias. However, there are channels that we can ask for help, assistance and advice from professional consultants or agencies, legal advisors, particular public or governmental authorities, and non-governmental organization (NGOs).

Fundamental requirements to establish a mutual understanding, beneficial relationships, or harmonious living and communications are: communicating or exchanging meaningful and useful messages; readiness to communicate; and showing respect and trust. Incomplete or ineffective communication, rebellious action, rejection, and ignorance or annoying behaviour are caused by: inappropriate manners or conduct; communication or relationship building by force or threat; misuse of messages for personal benefit or profit (insider trading); hiding, changing or giving false information; or denying of rights. Therefore, people should be given sufficient respect, space and choice after being involved in a proposed communication process.

5. **Speak only for ourselves by making more accurate statements.** Professionalism in effective interpersonal communication and relationship is determined by:

   a. The communicators understanding the reasons to commit into a communication process.
   b. The messages communicated being proper, complete, accurate and appropriate justifications to the feedback, responses, comments, reasoning, complaints, or suggestions.
   c. Having suitable and appropriate timing, avenue and agenda to communicate.

d. Using appropriate protocols to invite people, form groups, start the conversation or establish relationships.

e. Welcoming feedback, responses, comments, suggestions or solutions.

f. A talk, conversation, communication, demonstration, announcement, appointment, and decision making with proper, documented, or legalize permission, appointment or authority.

g. Pictures speak louder than words. Sometimes, the use of pictures and/or other audio-visual supporting materials such as samples, power-point presentations, and songs are more interesting and effective than speaking lengthy sentences, full of technical information.

h. Speak with confidence. Confidence in conversations may help to reduce speakers' nervousness or *stage-fright*. Add sufficient knowledge and preparation, staying focused on the talking-point, being alert and sensitive to the audiences' reactions and responses, and being able to control noises or interruptions.

6. **Speak but not too often or too long to avoid annoyance or misunderstanding**. Despite word, phrase or sentence arrangement, tone, tempo, and other physical factors (body gestures, movements, and distance) play a role to establish effective interpersonal communication. Besides, in public speaking, presentations or demonstrations, supporting materials, samples, machines and equipment are able to increase levels of understanding, acceptance and agreement from the listeners or audiences. Moreover, in order to create a beneficial, friendly and interesting conversation or interaction, communicators (both speakers and listeners) need to respect each other by talking or speaking appropriately and giving way to the others responses, then giving feedback, explanations, justifications, ideas, solutions or suggestions relevant to the topic of discussion. People who are "situation dominators"; speak too often, non-stop or too long; or have hygienic problems will break the audience's interest, attention and concentration, or cause annoyance, and boredom. Therefore, beneficial interpersonal relationships and

effective two-way communication is established through showing appropriateness, respect and sufficient skill in the art of speaking and listening.

7. **Challenge the behaviour and not the person, by avoiding personal comments or one sided communication**. Personal space is a person's comfort zone or areas of immediate surroundings which serve as psychological or emotional privacy and protection from threats from others (Dosey & Meisels, 1969). In addition, personal distance is a perceived space of a person's immediate surroundings, enforced in interpersonal interactions, especially with strangers or people from different cultural background, social status, hierarchy, and for hygienic or medical reasons (Little, 1965). Although there are no fixed geographical boundaries, the size of the preferred personal space or distance is determined by a person's personality, cultural background, intimacy level or mutual understanding between communicators.

In certain circumstances, people refuse to discuss the topic or message that brings personal meanings (ideas, feeling, perceptions or preferences), or uses language which is insulting or racist. Besides, inappropriate non-verbal reactions (eye contacts, body gestures and movements) may shows a sign of harassment, disturbance, rejection, ignorance, and annoyance, or interfere with personal space and distance. Nonetheless, it is very important for people to understand the appropriate space or distance to obtain respect, trust and effective communication participation.

There are sources, or experts such as psychiatrists and psychology counsellors which people can use for consultation, motivation, opinions, responses or advice. Therefore, effective interpersonal communication and relationship is established only when people are challenged, using reasonable and appropriate messages, about the behaviour but not the person, with mutual understanding or agreement. However, the high-context culture of Asia uses or incorporates personal issues in conversation even at the very first meeting with a stranger. This scenario creates discomfort or insecurity, especially among westerners. In fact, the reason for most Asians to talk about personal issues (such as by asking 'Did you take a bath this morning?', 'How much money do you earn every month?', 'Who else stays with you?') is just a way to start a friendly conversation or rapport (see, Awang-Rozaimie, Ali & Jaslin, 2010; Awang-Rozaimie, Ali, & Isma-Izza, 2010; Awang-Rozaimie, Ali, & Aiza, 2010).

8. **Respect confidentiality to gain mutual trust in beneficial relationship.** In addition to invading personal space and distance, there are messages that bring meanings (ideas, feeling or perceptions) that may harm the relationship and be dangerous to the personal, organization, society or national security, image, reputation or wealth. Some information is created, documented, recorded or transferred for personal, internal, protection or security reasons with a certain level of secrecy or confidentiality. For example, collected evidence or affidavits are stored with high police security and protection, especially in court jurisdictions of crime litigation. Only certain people or groups with particular authority are allowed to prepare, discuss or keep certain information before an official announcement, or exposure to the public domain. Hence, respecting confidentiality and secrecy are important to establish respect, trust and beneficial relationships.

9. **It is acceptable to make mistakes then learn from the mistake for improvement.** This statement is clear by itself in order to create a harmonious future and beneficial interpersonal relations and communication. In particular, mistakes are an inevitable, though inappropriate, misdirection of actions, behaviours or decisions. For example, in baking a cake, a burnt or improper shape, taste and look of the cake is probably caused by, inappropriate oven temperature or an incorrect recipe. Similarly, concerning interpersonal relations and communications, incomplete or broken relationships are probably caused by not following proper rules and regulations, procedures and protocols, or guidelines. There is an art in asking for forgiveness and apologizing for mistakes, by making appropriate promises, gift giving or making compensation. The mistakes can be used

as guidance to produce better works or establish beneficial relationships in the future.

Figure 11.1 summarizes the Emerson's basic principles to establish an effective interpersonal relationship and communication process. The seven principles are not mandatory, established or results in sequential but a salient knowledge to which people are unaware or insensitive.

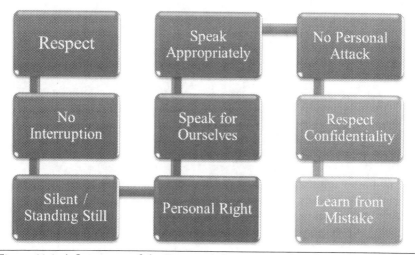

Figure 11.1: A Summary of the Emerson's Basic Principles of an Effective Relations and Communication Process

To conclude, this little book gives an insight or simple *rule of thumb* to create people awareness and sensitivity towards the establishment of effective and mutual interpersonal relations and communications. In addition, to have beneficial relations and effective communication, it is necessary for us to understand and acquire sufficient and appropriate knowledge and skills on how to manage and sustain the interpersonal communication and relationship process. Reflecting on these facts, we can see that the main reason for interpersonal interactions and communication creation is to obtain: feedback, responses, advice, comments, help or assistance; to feel appreciated, trusted and believed; to create intimacy; gain attention and loyalty; to stimulate interest and generate action and movement in decision making; or for effective relations (bringing out the best from oneself and gaining mutual trust from the others).

"The glory of friendship is not in the outstretched hand, nor the kindly smile, nor the joy of companionship; it is in the spiritual inspiration that comes to one when he discovers that someone else believes in him and is willing to trust him."

—Ralph Waldo Emerson—

References

Ainsworth, M. S., & Bowlby, J. (1991). An ethological approach to personality development. *American Psychologist, 46*(4), 333.

Ali, A. J., Van der Zee, K., & Sanders, G. (2003). Determinants of intercultural adjustment among expatriate spouses. *International Journal of Intercultural Relations, 27*(5), 563-580.

Awang-Rozaimie, A.S., Ali, A.J. & Dahlan, J. (2010), Match-made in Heaven: A Preliminary Study on Intercultural Understanding among Sojourners in Malaysia, *Academy of International Business (AIB) Southeast Asia Regional Conference*, 2nd-4th December 2010, Ho Chi Minh City, Vietnam.

Awang-Rozaimie, A.S., Ali, A.J. & Esa, I.I.M. (2010), Culture and Emotion Influence among Sojourners in Malaysia: A Preliminary Study, *3rd Asia-Euro Tourism, Hospitality & Gastronomy Conference 2010*, 24th-26th November 2010, Taylor's University College, Taylor's Lakeside Campus, Subang Jaya, Malaysia.

Awang-Rozaimie, A.S., Ali, A.J., & Johari, A. (2010), Intercultural Difficulties: Uncertainty Reduction by Sojourners in ASEAN Region, *International Conference on Management, Hospitality & Tourism (IMHA) 2010*, 12th-13th November 2010, BINUS University, Jakarta, Indonesia.

Bandura, A. (1977). Self-efficacy: Toward a unifying theory of behavioral change. *Psychological Review, 84*(2), 191-215.

Baxter, L. A., & Braithwaite, D. O. (2008). *Engaging theories in interpersonal communication: Multiple perspectives*: Sage.

Baxter, L. A., & Montgomery, B. M. (1996). *Relating: Dialogues and dialectics*: Guilford Press.

Black, J. S., Mendenhall, M., & Oddou, G. (1991). Toward a Comprehensive Model of International Adjustment: An Integrative of Multiple Theoritical Perspective. *Academy of Management Review, 16*(2), 291-317.

Bowlby, J. (1998). *Loss: Sadness and depression*: Random House.

Blumer, H. (1966). Sociological implications of the thought of George Herbert Mead. *American journal of sociology, 71*(5), 535.

Brewster, C., & Scullion, H. (1997). A review and agenda for expatriate HRM. *Human Resource Management Journal, 7*(3), 32-41.

Caligiuri, P. M. (1997). Assessing Expatriate Success: Beyond just 'Being There". *New Approaches to Employee Management* (Vol. 4, pp. 117-140). Greenwich: JAI Press Inc.

Claus, L., & Briscoe, D. (2009). Employee performance management across borders: A review of relevant academic literature. *International Journal of Management Reviews, 11*(2), 175-196.

Clark, M., & Hegel, G. W. F. (1971). *Logic and system*: Springer.

Costa, P., & McCrae, R. (1995). Domains and facets: Hierarchical personality assessment using the Revised NEO Personality Inventory. *Journal of Personality Assessment, 64*(1), 21-50.

DeVito, J. (2009), The Interpersonal Communication Book 12th ed. Allyn & Bacon (Pearson): Boston.

Daneman, M., & Carpenter, P. A. (1980). Individual differences in working memory and reading. *Journal of verbal learning and verbal behavior, 19*(4), 450-466.

Dosey, M. A. & Meisels, M. (1969). Personal space and self-protection. *Journal of Personality and Social Psychology*, 11(2), 93-97.

Emerson, R. W. (2010), http://www.communicationandconflict.com/interpersonal-communication.html [retrieved on 11th August 2010]

Forster, N. (1997). 'The persistent myth of high expatriate failure rates': a reappraisal. *International Journal of Human Resource Management, 8*(4), 414-433.

Friedman, P. A., Dyke, L. S., & Murphy, S. A. (2009). Expatriate adjustment from the inside out: An autoethnographic account. *International Journal of Human Resource Management, 20*(2), 252-268.

Giffin, K. (1967). The contribution of studies of source credibility to a theory of interpersonal trust in the communication process, *Psychological Bulletin*, 68 (2), 104-120.

Gross, J. J. (1998). Antecedent-and response-focused emotion regulation: divergent consequences for experience, expression, and physiology. *Journal of personality and social psychology, 74*(1), 224.

Gross, J. J. (2001). Emotion regulation in adulthood: Timing is everything. *Current directions in psychological science, 10*(6), 214-219.

Gross, J. J., & John, O. P. (2003). Individual differences in two emotion regulation processes: implications for affect, relationships, and well-being. *Journal of personality and social psychology, 85*(2), 348.

Gross, J. J., & Levenson, R. W. (1997). Hiding feelings: the acute effects of inhibiting negative and positive emotion. *Journal of abnormal psychology, 106*(1), 95.

Gudykunst, W. B. (1997). Cultural Variability in Communication: An Introduction. *Communication Research, 24*(4), 327-348.

Gudykunst, W. B. (2005). *An anxiety/uncertainty management (AUM) theory of strangers' intercultural adjustment.* In W. B. Gudykunst (Ed.), *Theorizing about intercultural communication,* 419-458. Thousand Oaks, California: Sage.

Hall, E. T. (1959). *The Silent Language.* New York: Anchor Press.

Harvey, S., & Goudvis, A. (2000). *Strategies that work: Teaching comprehension to enhance understanding* (Vol. 372): Stenhouse Publishers York, ME.

Harzing, A.-W. K. (1995). The persistent myth of high expatriate failure rates. *International Journal of Human Resource Management, 6*(2), 457-474.

Hofstede, G. (1983). The cultural relativity of organizational practices and theories. *Journal of International Business Studies, 14*(2), 75-89.

Hovland, C. I., & Weiss, W. (1951). The Influence of Source Credibility on Communication Effectiveness. *Public Opinion Quarterly, 15*(4), 635-650.

Kagan, J.D (1972). Do infants think? *Scientific American,* 226 (3), 71-82,

Kelly, G. A. (1955). The psychology of personal constructs (Vols. 1-2). New York: Norton.

Kilmann, R. H., & Thomas, K. W. (1977). Developing a forced-choice measure of conflict-handling behavior: The" MODE" instrument. *Educational and Psychological Measurement, 37*(2), 309-325.

Laub, J. H., Nagin, D. S., & Sampson, R. J. (1998). Trajectories of change in criminal offending: Good marriages and the desistance process. *American Sociological Review,* 225-238.

Lewis, P.S.: Goodman S.H. & Fandt, P.M. (2001). *Management: Challenges in the 21st Century,* 2nd edition, South-western.

Little, Kenneth B. (1965). Personal space. *Journal of Experimental Social Psychology,* 1(3), 1965, 237-247.

Martinko, M. J., & Douglas, S. C. (1999). Culture and expatriate failure: An attributional explication. *International Journal of Organizational Analysis, 7*(3), 265-293.

Maslow, A. H. (1943). A theory of human motivation. *Psychological review, 50*(4), 370.

Matsumoto, D. (2006). Are cultural differences in emotion regulation mediated by personality traits? *Journal of Cross-Cultural Psychology, 37*(4), 421-437.

Mayer, J. D., & Salovey, P. (1995). Emotional intelligence and the construction and regulation of feelings. *Applied and preventive psychology, 4*(3), 197-208.

Mayer, J. D., DiPaolo, M., & Salovey, P. (1990). Perceiving affective content in ambiguous visual stimuli: A component of emotional intelligence. *Journal of Personality Assessment, 54*(3-4), 772-781.

Mayfield, J., & Mayfield, M. (2002). Leader communication strategies critical paths to improving employee commitment. *American Business Review, 20*(2), 89-94.

Mayfield, J., & Mayfield, M. (2007). The effects of leader communication on a worker's intent to stay: An investigation using structural equation modelling. *Human Performance, 20*(2), 85-102.

Mendenhall, M., Stevens, M., Bird, A., & Oddou, G. (2008). Specification of the content domain of the Intercultural Effectiveness Scale. *The Kozai Monograph Series, 1*(2).

Montgomery, B. M., & Baxter, L. (1998). A guide to dialectical approaches to studying personal relationships. *Dialectical approaches to studying personal relationships,* 1-16.

Newsom. D, Turk J. V and Kruckeberg D, (2000). *This is PR: The Realities of Public Relations,* Seventh Edition, Belmont, Wadswoth/ Thomson Learning Press.

Nishida, H. (1999). A cognitive approach to intercultural communication based on schema theory. *International Journal of Intercultural Relations, 23*(5), 753-777.

Robinson, F. P. (1946). **Effective study.** NY: Harper & Brothers.

Salovey, P., & Mayer, J. D. (1990). Emotional intelligence. *Imagination, cognition and personality, 9*(3), 185-211.

Schutz, W.C. (2005). *The postulate of interpersonal needs: Description.* In S. Friedley, (Ed.). Foundations of interpersonal communication: A reader. (pp. 3-25). Reno, Nevada: Bent Tree Press.

Schultz. (1991). *FIRO theory of needs.* In W.C. Griffin, (Ed.). A first look at communication theory. Retrieved January 22, 2007, from http://www.afirstlook.com/archive/firo.pdf)

Searle, W., & Ward, C. (1990). The prediction of psychological and sociocultural adjustment during cross-cultural transitions. *International Journal of Intercultural Relations, 14*(4), 449-464.

Selmer, J. (2007). Which Is Easier, Adjusting to a Similar or to a Dissimilar Culture?: American Business Expatriates in Canada and Germany. *International Journal of Cross Cultural Management, 7*(2), 185-201.

Selmer, J., & Lauring, J. (2009). Cultural similarity and adjustment of expatriate academics. *International Journal of Intercultural Relations, 33*(5), 429-436.

Thibaut, J. & Kelley. H., (1959), The Social Psychology of Groups, NewYork:Wiley.

Thomas, K. W., & Kilmann, R. H. (1978). Comparison of four instruments measuring conflict behavior. *Psychological reports, 42*(3c), 1139-1145.

Ting-Toomey, S. & Takai, J. (2010). "Explaining Intercultural Conflict: Promising Approaches and Directions." *The SAGE Handbook of Conflict Communication.* 2006. SAGE Publications. 15 Apr. 2010.

Torbiorn, I. (1982). *Living abroad: Personal Adjustment and personnel policy in the overseas setting.* New York: John Wiley & Sons.

U.S. Census Bureau, http://www.census.gov/ipc/www/idb/worldgrgraph.php [retrieved on 11th August 2010]

Van Rooy, D. L., & Viswesvaran, C. (2004). Emotional intelligence: A meta-analytic investigation of predictive validity and nomological net. *Journal of Vocational Behavior, 65*(1), 71-95.

Ward, C., Bochner, S., & Furnham, A. (2001). *The Pschology of Culture Shock (2nd Edition).* East Sussex, England: Routledge.

Watzlawick, P., Beavin, J.H., & Jackson, D.D. (1967). Pragmatics of human communication: A study of interactional patterns, pathologies, and paradoxes, New York: W.W. Norton.

Whitchurch, G. G., & Constantine, L. L. (1993). Systems theory *Sourcebook of family theories and methods* (pp. 325-355): Springer.

_____ http://www.olc.org/diversity/adapt.html *[retrieved on 12th December 2010]*

_____ http://www.cse.iitk.ac.in/users/se367/11/se367/ganuj/project/proposal.html *[accessed on 2nd April 2014]*